No Safe Places

Death at the Hands of Illegal Aliens

NO SAFE PLACES

Death at the Hands of Illegal Aliens

Dave Gibson

THE SOCIAL CONTRACT PRESS
Petoskey, Michigan

Printed in the United States of America

First Printing, 2019

The Social Contract Press
445 E. Mitchell Street
Petoskey, Michigan 49770-2623

ISBN: 978-1-881780-39-7

For Benji and Margaret: you have made this life worth living.

CONTENTS

FOREWORD

The author asked Sabine Durden, a legal immigrant to this country, to write the foreword for No Safe Places: Death at the Hands of Illegal Aliens.

Sabine's only child, Dominic, or "Dom," was killed in 2012 by an illegal alien in California. Dominic was a dispatcher for the Riverside County Sheriff's Office, and was on his way to work when he was cut down at the age of 30.

Sabine has created a website, known as DOMHUGS (domhugs.com), *to not only bring attention to the needless tragedy that robbed her of her son, but also to educate others about this ongoing national tragedy, robbing so many fellow Americans of their loved ones.*

Dominic Durden's unfortunate story is on page 10 of this book.

Sabine's heartfelt and gracious words follow.

—D.G.

I found out about Dave Gibson's lifelong dedication to educate about and fight illegal immigration right after my only child, Dominic [see Dominic Durden, page 10], was killed on July 12, 2012, in California by an illegal alien who was no stranger to law enforcement and ICE (Immigration and Customs Enforcement). Dave not only answered many questions about my son's case, but helped me understand so much more about this issue, and while doing so, became a well-trusted and dear friend.

This book will wake you up and make you cry your eyes out, it will make you angry, very angry, it will break your heart. It will wake you up to this insanity, and it will make you question why you haven't heard more about these preventable tragedies in the mainstream media.

I am a legal immigrant from Germany and my only child, my son Dominic, was my heartbeat and my reason for living. He packed 100 years into his short life here on Earth and taught me to truly make every moment count, to live without regrets, and how to never take anyone or anything for granted.

I was blessed to have him with me for 30 wonderful years, and the memories of those times with him keep my broken heart smiling and keep me going. Because of his death and the forever separation and destruction of my family, I became a fighter and advocate against illegal immigration, to make sure that my son will never be forgotten and that no other family has to feel the pain and grief that, sadly, many others now also know.

This book will keep you captivated, and if you haven't lost a loved one because of this issue, you will still be able to relate to and understand the senselessness of those untimely and preventable deaths. It will make you hug your loved ones a little tighter and never take a moment for granted. It will make you appreciate your life a lot more.

I thank you, Dave Gibson, for allowing me to be a part of your effort to bring awareness, knowledge, understanding, and even a little peace to those who experienced these permanent losses. *No Safe Places: Death at the Hands of Illegal Aliens* is an extraordinary gift to anyone who reads it.

With huge Domhugs from Dom's mom, Sabine!

INTRODUCTION

On August 21, 2018, Cristhian Bahena Rivera, 24, led police to the body of 20-year-old Mollie Tibbetts, a University of Iowa student who had been missing for more than a month. Her body had been left in a cornfield, covered in leaves and debris.

Rivera told investigators that he saw the young woman jogging, and began to follow her in his vehicle. Eventually he exited his Chevy Malibu and began running alongside her.

According to court documents, Mollie then told her assailant that she was calling the police.

Under questioning, Rivera claimed that he had then "blacked out" and could not remember how Mollie's bloody, lifeless body came to be in the trunk of his car. He however admitted taking her body from the trunk and hiding it in the cornfield. The Iowa State Medical Examiner's preliminary autopsy revealed that the victim had died from "multiple sharp force injuries."

Rivera, an illegal alien from Mexico, had been living in the area where Mollie's abduction and murder took place for four to seven years, according to police.

Later that same evening, President Trump said this at an event in West Virginia:

> You heard about today with the illegal alien coming in, very sadly, from Mexico. And you saw what happened to that incredible, beautiful young woman. Should have never happened. Illegally in our country. We've had a huge impact but the laws are so bad, the immigration laws are such a disgrace. We're getting it changed, but we have to get more Republicans.

While Mollie's abduction and murder drew national attention, the deaths of thousands of other Americans at the hands of illegal aliens have not.

This book contains 50 chapters, each devoted to the case of at least one of those *other victims*, whose untimely and often brutal deaths were largely or altogether ignored by the national press. Many of these chapters include heart-breaking interviews with the victims' family members.

The cases in these chapters are a small sample of a database author Dave Gibson has compiled through years of research on crimes committed by illegal immigrants to the U.S. The ages of the victims in this sample range from newborn to ninety-three, their deaths occuring in at least twenty states at the hands of criminals from nearly as many countries.

A freelance writer and former legislative aide to a Virginia State Senator, Dave Gibson is a featured contributor to *The Social Contract*, a quarterly journal of public affairs. He makes his home in Virginia. The focus of his research and writing is exclusively on the topic of illegal immigration and the crimes committed by those who have no legal right to be on American soil. His website (illegalaliencrimereport.com) features daily reports on those crimes, including murders, rapes, child sexual assaults, as well as several other crimes, now plaguing American cities large and small.

As Gibson often vociferously states: "Unlike all other crimes, the ones perpetrated by illegal aliens are 100 percent preventable...It's really very simple: if they are not here, *they are not here to commit the crime!*"

1

Tessa Tranchant and Alison Kunhardt

Ages: 16 and 17 respectively
Location of Death: Virginia Beach, Virginia
Killer: Alfredo Ramos

On March 30, 2007, a Mexican national named Alfredo Ramos slammed his car into the rear of a vehicle in which Alison Kuhnhardt, 17, and Tessa Tranchant, 16, were sitting, while waiting at a traffic light.

Ramos, 22, was traveling at least 65 mph, when he hit the Plymouth Duster, and had a blood alcohol concentration (BAC) of .24 (three times the legal limit of a DUI), according to court documents.

The two high school students had to be cut from their crumpled car and both died a short time after being transported to the hospital. Ramos suffered only a busted lip. Tessa's brother, Dylan, was tasked with identifying his little sister's body.

Dylan, a Marine, had only been home from Iraq for two weeks when his sister was killed.

Ramos had been living in Virginia Beach for quite a while and worked at a local Mexican restaurant known as Mi Casita. He was previously convicted of three separate charges of public intoxication and identity theft as well as a DUI.

Despite his criminal history and illegal status in this country, Ramos was never reported to federal immigration officials, and continued to live in the area. He speaks only Spanish and required an interpreter at all of his court proceedings.

The case gained national fame thanks to the reporting of Fox News' Bill O'Reilly, who called Virginia Beach a "sanctuary city" for illegal aliens.

O'Reilly placed the blame on that city's Mayor Meyra Obendorf and Police Chief Jake Jacocks, and characterized the resort town as a place where foreign criminals were allowed to roam freely.

Chief Jake Jacocks went on the offensive and claimed that O'Reilly was wrong in focusing on the fact that Ramos was an illegal alien. He accused the Fox News commentator of turning the girls' deaths into a "political issue."[1]

However, shortly after the girls were killed, information on how the Virginia Beach Police Department deals with illegal aliens came to light.

"A 2005 Virginia Beach Police Department policy forbids officers from asking the immigration status of defendants charged with misdemeanors. Police Chief Jake Jacocks, Jr. has said the policy is meant to encourage illegal aliens to report crimes without fear of retribution," the *Washingtom Times* reported.[2]

Ramos pleaded guilty to two counts of aggravated involuntary manslaughter and was sentenced to 24 years in prison and ordered to be deported upon his release.

Minutes before Ramos was sentenced, Alison's dad, David Kunhardt, had a very blunt message for the man who killed his daughter.

> If I were to have one wish, it is that Alfredo Ramos would have to visit Ali and Tessa at Princess Anne Memorial Park Cemetery for the rest of his life.

In 2010, Tessa's dad, Ray Tranchant, penned an op-ed for Fox News about his daughter's death.[3]

> My 16-year-old daughter, Tessa, was killed by an illegal immigrant in Virginia Beach three years ago while sitting at a stop light. Her friend Ali Kunhardt, 17, also perished instantly.

Beautiful girls with tons of future plans, they had just stopped at a convenience store for a pack of gum at 10 on a Friday night. I can imagine that they were giggling about something as they waited for the red light to turn green. Tessa was in the passenger seat. I'll never forget her laugh.

The explosion was so loud that witnesses said it sounded like a bomb going off, hit from behind by a black Mitsubishi going more than 70 mph. They were tiny, skinny little girls stuffed somewhere in the floorboards when the police and EMT crew arrived.

When I got to the hospital in what seemed like a dream sequence, Tessa's bed was lying next to Ali's, separated by a privacy curtain. Both girls were perfectly still, skin cold to the touch.

Tess was covered with a hospital blanket, and her clothes lay in a bag by her bedside, cut off by the EMT and the ER doctor who tried to revive her, to no avail. I looked at her large brown eyes, pupils dilated, eyes wide open, staring at the ceiling. She still had a mask taped to her mouth with a long rubber tube. The center of the tube was filled with bright red blood. Amazingly, she had only a little bruise on her forehead, and her big toe was bleeding. I noticed that she had had a couple of her nails done with glitter, probably had just enough money to do two. She worked at the Golden Corral; Ali worked at The Fresh Market.

I hadn't seen Tessa in a few days, and I had to laugh at her forearm. Hard to believe you can laugh with such horror around you, but I did. She had previously told me that she suffered from the "Tranchant curse" — dark hair on her skinny little perfect arms — and apparently she had shaved it all off (her way of getting even, I guess).

Alfredo Ramos, a previous DUI offender and alcoholic, seemed invisible in a system that was good at looking the other way. Virginia Beach and Chesapeake were being accused of being "sanctuary cities" as Bill O'Reilly and Geraldo Rivera screamed at each other during the national news hour. O'Reilly was right.

I know what sanctuary means more than most ever will....

We don't share a border with Mexico, so the awareness here isn't as great as Arizona or California.

A few months after his daughter's untimely death, Ray Tranchant sat down for a brief interview:

Q: *How are you and your family coping with this terrible loss?*

A: It is the biggest challenge of my life. I have been through some hard but fun times being a retired Naval officer, Annapolis graduate, Aircraft Carrier aviator, public school teacher, and now College administrator. The challenges these career paths have taken me pale in comparison to losing a little girl.

If you have suffered a loss of someone close to you that is totally unexpected (death sometimes is more predictable with serious illnesses, age, or severe accidents), no matter what the reason, it is at first almost surreal.

My ex-wife Colette, Kelsey (15), and Dylan (25) were swept with total emotion and grief immediately, and I chose to compartmentalize and suppress my grief so that the tasks at hand (funeral arrangements, family, and my job) were taken care of. I suffer still, but need help from friends and God to cope.

Colette still understandably breaks down a lot and Kelsey is angry about many things in life that I don't think would have bothered her if her sister were still alive. Dylan moved away from the area and chose to go to a College in Washington, D.C. about 200 miles from Virginia Beach. He is an artist and will undoubtedly express himself with music and drawings. All of us are undergoing therapy and need various medications.

Q: *What kind of kid was Tessa?*

A: Tessa was a free spirit, and had many gifts, like emotional intelligence. She was very attractive and was everyone's friend (a social animal that got up at 4:00 am in the morning to get ready for High School), a gifted Irish step dancer, and a good surfer, had a great voice, and tickled me with her laugh. She loved comedies; anything with Ben Stiller, Will Farrell, Dave Chappell, Mike Myers, and Borat.

When she smiled, my heart always skipped a beat. She was truly loved by everyone who spent any time with her.

She is buried next to her friend Ali Kunhardt in Princess Anne Memorial Park, next to a statue of an angel. I visit her every Friday, since the night she was killed.

The crash site on Virginia Beach Blvd. continues to be a memorial by the community, it always has flowers, balloons, notes, and pictures.

Q: *Did you ever see Alfredo Ramos display any remorse for his crime? And what would you say to him?*

A: No and I have a feeling that is why Judge Shadrick gave him 40 years in prison.

Q: *Do you feel that the circumstances of your daughter's death have been accurately reported by the media?*

A: I think the media has done a good job reporting the facts. I think that Fox News, O'Reilly, Glenn Beck on MSNBC, and Laura Ingraham on Fox were very gracious in letting me tell our story. When the deaths happened, Virginia Beach seemed more worried about the mudslinging with O'Reilly than admitting that the system was broken and change needed to be on the horizon.

Q: *How has this tragedy changed your life?*

A: I am more compassionate with my fellow man, I walk and talk to God more often and with more conviction, and I try to look at the big picture more than I used to before the deaths. I try not to get bogged down with the small details that won't matter in the long run, and finally, I see how fragile life really is.

Alfredo Ramos is currently housed at the Greensville Correctional Center in Jarratt, Virginia, and has a scheduled release date of March 14, 2028, according to the Virginia Department of Corrections.[4]

2

Joe Storie

Age: 51
Location of Death: Kill Devil Hills, North Carolina
Killer: Luis Alberto Rodriguez

On October 5, 2011, Luis Alberto Rodriguez, 44, sped through a flashing red light at the intersection of Colington Road and U.S. 158 in Kill Devil Hills, and crashed his Chevy Lumina into the pickup truck driven by Paul Davis. The truck was hit with such force that it flipped over, killing 51-year-old Joe Storie, a passenger in the vehicle, according to court documents.

Two other passengers, Joe's wife, Alicia Storie, and his sister, Chris Storie, were both critically injured in the wreck and were taken to Norfolk General Hospital in Virginia by air ambulance.

Rodriguez was taken to the same hospital with serious injuries. Incredibly, days later, Rodriguez walked out of that same hospital, embarking on what would be only his first flight from justice.

The *Outer Banks Voice* reported:

> Sources within the Kill Devil Hills Police Department told the Voice they requested aid from the Norfolk Police Department to ensure Rodriguez did not leave the hospital. But they were informed that Norfolk could not spare the manpower, although the state would argue later that there were Norfolk police officers stationed at the hospital.[1]

Police called Sentara Norfolk General every day while Rodriguez was a patient to check on his recovery and were told, "he is in no condition to walk out of here" each time.

Kill Devils Hills police, along with other agencies, eventually tracked the criminal alien to the state capital (and "sanctuary city") of Raleigh, and brought him back to Dare County.

Rodriguez was charged with one count of felony death by vehicle, two counts of serious injury by vehicle, and one count of driving while impaired.

The illegal alien claimed poverty, was appointed a public defender, and a secured bond was set at $100,000. Despite the fact that he was in the country illegally and claimed to be "without assets," on January 9, 2012, Rodriguez appeared before Dare County District Judge J.C. Cole, with his own, hired lawyer, for a second bond reduction hearing (after an initial hearing saw District Judge Edgar Barnes uphold the higher bail amount).

His defense attorney, Phillip Hayes, said of his client:

> ...his evidence of risk of flight. I submit is little or none, and the fact that he does have connections to Dare County, a residence in Dare County, family in Dare County. For all intents and purposes he is a citizen of Dare County and he's not going anywhere, Judge.

Apparently, Judge Cole was impressed by the illegal alien's "family values" and actually reduced the secured bail amount to $50,000. Rodriguez found a bondsman and was released with a pending court date of April 23, 2012. Rodriguez failed to show for court and the illegal alien is still a fugitive.

What follows is an an interview with Joe's sister, Chris Storie, who bore witness to her own brother's painful death, and who, herself, was badly injured that fateful night:

Q: *When did you find out that your brother had passed away?*

A: I found out about my brother's death after my family back home did. They would not tell me anything. I kept asking for Joey and telling them to call him for me. He was always my protector and I needed him there with me. Hours after I woke up they sent a chaplain in and I knew before she even opened her mouth. It still does not seem real.

Q: *When did you find out that the illegal alien had escaped the hospital?*

A: After I got back home from Norfolk hospital, Officer Tatterson from the Kill Devil Hills Police Department called and told me that Luis Rodriguez was under 24-hour watch to make sure he did not leave the hospital. Later we learned he was never under any kind of watch after all and he fled the hospital.

Q: *What is your opinion of the police and prosecutor?*

A: It was the Kill Devil Hills Police Department (KDHPD), and I was told lie after lie. Chief Britt stood my sisters up for a meeting we had scheduled with him after we had driven seven hours to meet with him. Then he would not take my calls. After I gave a fake name he came right to the phone and was not very nice at all when he found out it was me.

The Assistant District Attorney, Christen Simmons, was horrible! She treated me terribly and did not do a good job at the second bond reduction hearing. Judge Barnes was the judge in the first hearing and did not reduce the bond because he said Rodriguez was a proven flight risk. The second judge, Judge Cole, reduced it from $100,000 to $50,000. We later found out his wife is an attorney who defends illegal immigrants. Luis of course fled again. He came up with approximately $13,000 to get away. There is so much more I could tell you, but it would take days or weeks.

Q: *What injuries did you suffer in the crash?*

A: I had a massive head injury, neck injury, and many cuts on my feet and legs. My whole body was one huge bruise. The mental part has been the worst though. I now have PTSD (Post Traumatic Stress Disorder), survivors guilt, and depression. I had surgery on my neck August 14, 2014, because the injury to my neck worsened over time and a disc was pressing into my spine. I'm out of work again for awhile. I missed five and a half months initially from the crash, then two more months when I went in the mental hospital, now three months for another surgery. I have always been a very strong, determined person, but this really sent me reeling. Losing my brother is the hardest thing I have ever gone through. For my family as well.

Q: *What would you like everyone to know about this tragedy?*
A: The man who has devastated my family showed no remorse whatsoever about killing Joey. He is illegal, fled twice, and I truly believe he had help from our so-called justice system in getting away.

He had the opportunity to apologize and say he was sorry to mine and Joey's sons, but he didn't. The illegal (expletive) should have never been in this country to start with! He had just gotten a ticket two months prior to this crash for running a red light! If this had been an American citizen, he would have been held accountable as he should be. The KDHPD had the nerve to tell me it was *their* culture to drink and drive. I told them that they need to keep their culture and their (expletive) in their own country! Not bring it to *ours*!

The Dare County Community Crime Line has offered a reward of $1,000 for information leading to the capture of Luis Alberto Rodriguez, and the Storie family has put up an additional $1,000. Anyone with information on the whereabouts of this fugitive is asked to call the Crime Line at (252) 473-3111 or (800) 745-2746.

Investigators believe Rodriguez may be living in Tennessee, the Raleigh/Durham area, or Honduras.

3

Dominic Durden

Age: 30
Location of Death: Riverside County, California
Killer: Juan Zacarias Lopez Tzun

On July 12, 2012, Dominic Durden, a 30-year-old Riverside County, California sheriff's dispatcher, was on his way to work, when Juan Zacarias Lopez Tzun, 24, made an illegal left-hand turn in his pickup on Pigeon Pass Road, striking Durden's motorcycle. Durden's injuries were massive and he died at the scene.

Tzun, an illegal alien, was charged with vehicular manslaughter and for driving without a license. Despite the fact that Tzun killed an innocent young man, he was booked into the Robert Presley Jail in Riverside, on only $7,500 bail.

On April 3, 2013, Riverside County Superior Court Judge Raphael A. Arreola sentenced Tzun to 90 days in jail and to 180 days in a work-release program. Tzun had already spent 56 days in jail, and only served an additional 30 days, before being released on May 2, after which, he was eventually deported.

Not surprisingly, the crash that killed Durden was not Tzun's first run-in[1] with the law...what follows is Tzun's criminal history in California:

- On May 13, 2012, he was arrested and charged with

suspicion of driving under the influence and not having a license.

• In November 2010, he pleaded guilty to driving under the influence and was sentenced to three years' probation, 10 days in jail, and a $1,660 fine. Under the terms of his probation, he was required to obtain a driver's license...he never did.

• In 2009, he was charged with grand theft auto.

Despite these charges, Tzun was never reported to U.S. Immigration and Customs Enforcement (ICE) officials for possible deportation, and was allowed to roam freely, continuing to place the citizens of Riverside County in grave danger.

In fact, *The Riverside Press-Enterprise* reported that the California Highway Patrol refused to investigate Tzun's immigration status, following his first DUI arrest.[2]

Furthermore, the paper also reported:

> The Riverside County Sheriff's Department does not inform ICE of impending releases after receiving an immigration detainer, Sgt. Mike Manning said.[3]

In addition to serving as a sheriff's 911 dispatcher, Durden was a volunteer firefighter and an accomplished pilot. "Dom," as his mother, Sabine called him, loved animals and was the "ultimate prankster, ...who would do anything to make you laugh."

It was Durden's lifelong dream to become a police officer, and he spent much of his 30 years on Earth helping others and bringing a smile to the faces of his friends and family.

Sabine Durden agreed to sit down for an interview for this project, in which she asked about the impact of Dominic's untimely death and the incredibly unjust circumstances surrounding it. Her heartfelt and inspiring words can also be found on the website she created to honor her son's memory, known as DOMHUGS.[4]

Her words follow:

Q: *Can you describe what life was like with your son, "Dom?"*

A: Dominic was my only child, my best friend, the love of my life, the best friend of so many and an incredible human being.

In his short 30 years of life, he accomplished more than some people do in a lifetime. He was named Volunteer of the Year 2004 in our City, managed to get his Private Pilot license, and rescued his beloved Cyrus from the pound.

His motorcycle, traveling, and hanging out with friends were very important to him, and even though he led a very busy life, he was never too busy to spend time with me. I now have 30 years of wonderful memories of times spent together.

Dominic was also known to be the most dependable and reliable friend, coworker, and also the kind of man every parent would want for a son in law.

My sweet son lived life to the fullest and truly enjoyed life as if he knew he wouldn't be around for a long time.

His sense of humor was second to none, his deep and contagious laugh and his photo bombing bug eyes became his trademark. Many people, including me, became victims of his pranks, and many stories are still being shared and fondly remembered.

Dom's best prank was one that involved a local Police Officer that helped him pull off the ultimate prank of all times. He arranged for that Officer to pull him over as he was on his way to the airport to go flying with a friend [Tom] who visited from out of town. The Officer pulled them over and after some questioning of who, what, and where, he asked Dominic to step out of the truck and handcuffed him.

Tom was visibly shaking and upset as the officer asked him where they were heading to. He shared that they were on their way to the airport to go flying and the Officer replied: "oh, is that what they call it now? Do you know he is the best known and busiest male prostitute known around here? You are under arrest."

As poor Tom was about to lose it and pass out, Dominic and the Officer busted out laughing so hard and could barely stand up any longer.

This prank and so many others he pulled on unsuspecting friends will always put a huge smile on all of our faces and broken hearts.

Dominic taught all of us to enjoy every moment in life. He made us realize to live and love to the fullest, seize every moment, and most of all, live without regrets.

He will never be forgotten and his presence is still felt by many who knew him.

I miss my "German Chocolate" son and his great Domhugs.

Q: *Has the loss of your son changed you?*

A: My answer is *yes* and *no.*

When Dominic was killed that horrific day on July 12, 2012, I knew I would never be the same. I knew I was forever changed and had to come to grips with a new reality. A new way of life without the most important person in it.

I realized that I could just slowly die or that I could make a difference and continue my amazing son's legacy. The choice was easy. There was no way I would let his death be in vain.

There are many days that I can barely breathe and the pain of missing Dominic is so intense that it takes every bit of strength to make it. I also learned to be a great actress and hide my pain, put on a smile, and crack a joke.

No matter what, I knew I just had to continue and be Dominic's voice. After all, I was all he had left.

July 10, 2015, I got to meet Donald Trump in Beverly Hills, and after sharing my story with him privately, I had the chance to share Dominic's story with the world at a press conference set up by Mr. Trump.

My life changed even more after that. More news stations were now suddenly interested in what happened to my only child, and I took advantage of every chance to share who Dominic was and why he was no longer alive.

A few visits to Washington, D.C., starting Twitter (@Sabine_Durden) posts, a few more interviews on TV and radio stations, and a lot more knowledge about politics became my "new Life."

Yes, I have changed.

No, I am not better. The pain will never go away and my heart is forever broken.

I could have stopped living after Dominic's death. I could have just let life go by. But I chose to share my experience, connect with other victims of illegal alien crime, speak up and get active. I became a voice for many who can't or are not able to speak up.

Sadly, some people who were in my life didn't appreciate it or like what and who I was talking about.

Some disappeared, some tried to change my way of thinking and talking. They wanted to change who I became and didn't like or understand the why and how.

While I lost some, I gained a lot of new friends and supporters that are by my side no matter what.

No matter what tragedy happens to us, we have a choice how we continue after it happens. Will it stop us from living or will it make us stronger?

I found out so much about me, my strength, and just how resilient I am.

My sweet Dominic lets me know in many ways that he is around and very proud of his mom. I honor my son by continuing to share his story and be his voice.

While I make sure his legacy continues, I am also making sure that people will get to know *DOMSMOM.*

Never take a moment with your loved ones for granted and make sure they know how you feel.

Sabine Durden has established a scholarship in Dominic's name to assist students enrolled in Emergency Medical Technician programs at Moreno Valley College.[5]

Unlike President Obama's so-called "DREAMERS," who, in reality, are nothing more than criminals, Dominic Durden was a true "dreamer" who also put those dreams into action (he achieved a 4.0 GPA, became a pilot, and always donated his time to his community...all by the age of 30!). His death is a loss, not only to those who were fortunate to have known him personally, but to every American.

"Dom" was a young man whom all of us would be proud to call brother, son, or pal.

So, go ahead and weep for this true "dreamer!"

4

Marten Kudlis

Age: 3
Location of Death: Aurora, Colorado
Killer: Francis Hernandez

On September 10, the parents of 3-year-old Marten Kudlis buried their son at Fairmount Cemetery, after he was killed while waiting for his ice cream in a Denver-area Baskin and Robbins.

An SUV speeding through the intersection of Havana and Mississippi, with Guatemalan national Francis Hernandez at the wheel, slammed into a pickup truck, which was then pushed into the ice cream shop's window. The toddler was sitting at a table in front of that window, and was sent flying as the truck came crashing through it.

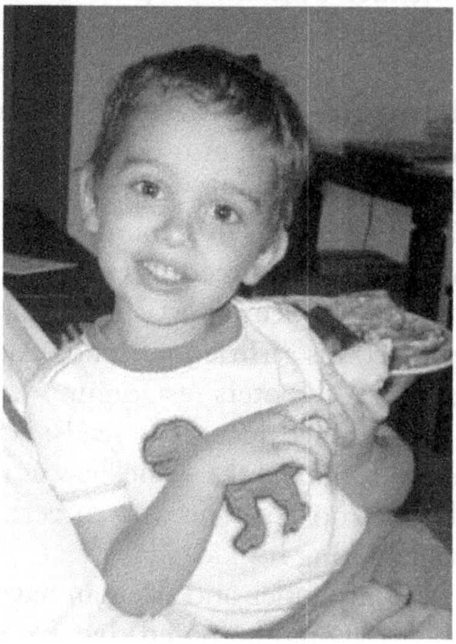

After the crash, Hernandez jumped from his Chevy Suburban and fled the scene. He was later apprehended without incident.

Marten was taken to the hospital, but died a short time later due to massive internal injuries.

The two women in the pickup truck struck by Hernandez were Patricia Guntharp, 49, and Debra Serecky, 51. They were both pronounced dead at the scene.

The Denver Channel covered the child's funeral and reported that the first song heard during the service was Eric Clapton's "Tears in Heaven."[1]

In a heart-wrenching display of grief and anger, Marten's mother Marat Kudlis shouted: "That bastard!", referring to the illegal immigrant who killed her son. Between the tears, Marten's father cried out: "I really loved him."

The rabbi conducting the service told the heartbroken family and friends: "This burden feels like more than we can bear because it is so sudden. It's a parent's worst nightmare. It does not seem fair and it is not fair to lose someone so young."

A teddy bear was placed in the tiny open casket which held Marten's body.

Following the funeral, many of the mourners returned to the crash site, which has become a makeshift memorial, filled with flowers, stuffed animals, and cards with expressions of sympathy and support for the Kudlis family.

One of those mourners, Duane Stokes, told a KMGH reporter: "I helped pull Marten out of the building. I was right there with him. He squeezed my hand. I held his hand until he passed on. My fiance and I were just saying a prayer to Marten and just getting one last glimpse of everything around here. Just to say goodbye to him."

Marten's death hit the community hard and his funeral was attended by many people who never met him, but were both saddened and angered by his senseless death.

Hernandez, who had no less than 12 aliases and two dates of birth, had been arrested 19 times since 2003. The Colorado Bureau of Investigation also confirmed that Hernandez had been arrested by nine different police departments. Despite his lengthy arrest record and illegal status in this country, Hernandez was never deported nor were deportation proceedings ever started against him.

The police report shows that Hernandez ran from the scene and phoned his girlfriend, Brenda Aleman, asking her to come pick him up at a local Hooters restaurant.

A court document reads: "(He) stated after the accident he was scared and fled the scene, he was afraid he would be taken to jail because he had no insurance, no driver's license, and that would prevent him from seeing his kids."[2]

Hernandez and Aleman have an infant and a 2-year-old.

It should be noted that Denver is officially a "sanctuary city." The term refers to a policy taken by cities which refuse to inquire into an arrestee's immigration status, or a refusal to inform federal authorities when a suspect in custody is believed or known to be an illegal alien.

A few days after the deadly crash, Colorado Republican Congressman and former presidential candidate Tom Tancredo said that then-Denver Mayor John Hickenlooper, as well as then-Colorado Gov. Bill Ritter, "have blood on their hands."

While both Hickenlooper and Ritter have long been criticized for their opposition to tough enforcement of our immigration laws, Ritter tried to deflect any attention from his office onto the federal government and called Tancredo's comments "out of bounds."

Rep. Tancredo issued the following statement:

"While it might be politically expedient to blame Washington for what happened this week or to characterize my criticism of him as 'out of bounds,' the fact remains that Gov. Ritter is in charge of enforcing and keeping Coloradans safe. It's time for Gov. Ritter to take concrete steps to ensure that illegal aliens like Francis Hernandez, who had been apprehended by police more than a dozen times, end up behind bars, not back behind the wheel."

5

Dr. Edward Horowitz

Age: 64
Location of Death: Omaha, Nebraska
Killer: Pedro Diego-Antonio

On June 22, 2014, police in Omaha arrested Pedro Diego-Antonio, 31, after he hit a man crossing the street at the intersection of 38th and Dodge Streets. The Guatemalan national fled the scene, but was taken into custody only a few blocks from the fatal crash.

As a result of the impact, the victim, 64-year-old Dr. Edward Horowitz, was thrown nearly 20 feet, into the windshield of a U-Haul truck stopped at the red light. Less than an hour later, he died at a local hospital from his massive injuries.

Diego-Antonio, who had a .24 Blood Alcohol Concentration (BAC), more than three times the legal limit at the time of the accident, was charged with vehicular homicide, felony DUI causing serious bodily injury or death, and felony leaving the scene of an accident. He was booked into the Douglas County Corrections Center on an Immigration and Customs Enforcement (ICE) detainer.

Diego-Antonio was stopped and cited only 11 days before the fatal DUI, for driving on a suspended license. In fact, it was the second time that year that the illegal alien was ticketed for driving without a license, after being convicted of a 2011 DUI.

"Diego-Antonio, who had a DUI in 2011, had drunk between 15 and 20 beers and was barreling west on Dodge Street," reported The Omaha World Herald.[1]

While common sense dictates that he should have been deported after the first DUI, in 2012, President Obama ordered ICE agents to stop detaining and ordering the deportation of illegal aliens charged with a single misdemeanor.[2]

Among the conditions under which ICE agents were then permitted to issue a detainer was if "the individual has three or more prior misdemeanor convictions."

Since Diego-Antonio's prior DUI was apparently discounted, it would have taken one more citation for driving without a license for him to have even received a deportation hearing.

As for the victim, Creighton University, where he worked, released the following statement:

> Creighton University School of Medicine mourns the unexpected loss of Edward Horowitz, M.D., an associate professor of medicine in the Division of Infectious Diseases who also held a secondary appointment in the Department of Medical Microbiology & Immunology.
>
> Horowitz was a passionate educator and, as such, has touched the lives of countless medical students during his tenure at Creighton University. His loss weighs heavy on the hearts of faculty, staff, and students within the medical school and across the campus. As a community, we grieve with his family and friends and we offer our heartfelt support for his closest colleagues and collaborators.
>
> Horowitz, born in Los Angeles, Calif., in 1950, started a nearly four-decades-long career at Creighton University as a medical student. He graduated from the School of Medicine in 1978 before completing an internship,

> residency, chief residency, and a fellowship in infectious diseases — all at Creighton University Affiliated Hospitals.
>
> Once named a 'Best Doctor in America,' Horowitz practiced at the VA Medical Center as well as the Creighton Travel Clinic at Alegent Creighton Clinic in Dundee. He also provided care to the community as a staff physician at the Omaha Indian-Chicano Health Center in the 1980s, La Plaza Health Center in the 1990s, and at the Magis Clinic at Sienna Francis House since 2001.[3]

In April 2015, Douglas County District Judge Shelly Stratman sentenced Diego-Antonio to 35 to 40 years in state prison. However, due to Nebraska state law, the illegal alien will likely only serve 17 to 20 years of that sentence.

6

Officer Rodney Johnson

Age: 40
Location of Death: Houston, Texas
Killer: Juan Leonardo Quintero

On September 21, 2006, Officer Johnson was shot and killed while making a routine traffic stop. The man who murdered Officer Johnson was a Mexican national who had been deported seven years earlier.

Officer Johnson stopped a commercial vehicle traveling 20 miles over the posted speed limit. The truck was driven by Juan Leonardo Quintero. A co-worker and Quintero's two stepdaughters were also in the vehicle.

When Quintero was unable to provide any form of identification, Officer Johnson handcuffed him and placed him in the backseat of his patrol car. Once Johnson was seated behind the wheel again, Quintero, though handcuffed, removed the 9mm handgun concealed in his waistband and began firing at Johnson through the plastic shield separating the front and back seats.

Officer Johnson was shot in the head five times. He was pronounced dead on arrival at a local hospital.

Juan Leonardo Quintero had prior arrests in Houston. He is a convicted child molester and DUI offender. He had been working for a Houston area landscaping company and, despite the DUI conviction, was driving a company vehicle at the time Officer Johnson stopped him.

Clara Rodriguez, who lived in the neighborhood where Johnson patrolled, had this to say about the murdered officer:

> He was just so very nice. He was not ever mean. It just breaks my heart. I feel so very bad for his wife. He got up and went to work this morning, and this is what happened. This is what happened to one of the people who protects us, who truly took care of us. [1]

On May 20, 2008, a Houston jury sentenced Quintero to spend the rest of his life in prison.

The owner of the landscaping firm who hired Quintero was also indicted by a federal grand jury. In 2009, Robert Lane Camp pleaded guilty to harboring an illegal alien.[2]

Forty-year-old Officer Rodney Johnson was a 12-year veteran of the Houston Police Department (HPD) and a U.S. Army veteran. While serving on the HPD, Johnson received two Lifesaving Awards. He left behind his wife, Joslyn (also a police officer), and five children. [3]

Of course, Houston was at the time of Ofc. Johnson's murder, and remains today, a "sanctuary city" for illegal aliens.

7

April Lee Sweet

Age: 7
Location of Death: Alexander County, North Carolina
Killer: Bernardino Zuniga

On July 13, 1982, the body of 7-year-old April Lee Sweet was found several hours after she had gone missing from her grandparent's Alexander County home, in rural North Carolina. The little girl had been stabbed in the neck and left naked from the waist down, her shorts and underwear lying next to her. An autopsy confirmed that the rising second-grader had been raped.

Earlier that day, April's grandfather, Calvin Johnson, spoke to her for what would be the last time as he walked out of his home and joined the rest of his family to work their tobacco fields. While driving his pickup truck in the fields, he noticed a taxi coming down the road, and the man riding in the backseat was a man he knew as "Richard Lopez," a migrant farm worker.

Lopez had actually worked for Johnson in the past, and Johnson even invited the man who spoke very little English into his home on a few occasions. This man, who took Johnson's granddaughter from him, would later be identified as Bernadino Zuniga.

Around noon, Johnson returned to the house to find April missing. Panicked, he phoned the Alexander County Sheriff's Department, while his wife and the girl's parents continued searching for her.

Johnson told Sheriff Thomas E. Bebber that he had seen Lopez in a cab, headed towards his property a few hours earlier. The sheriff issued a BOLO alert for a Mexican male "approximately 5 foot 9, 155 pounds, wearing blue jeans, a blue or gray shirt."

As it turned out, Zuniga took another cab to the bus station after murdering April and headed to Pine Bluff, Arkansas. He was taken into custody in Knoxville, Tennessee.

The arrest affidavit was graphic and painted a clear picture of what happened to the little girl.

> At the police station in Knoxville, officers took hair and fingernail scrapings from the defendant. As defendant took down his trousers for a pubic hair sample, Detective Moyer noticed that defendant pulled both trousers and underpants down simultaneously. Later, having become suspicious, Detective Moyer asked to see defendant's undershorts. The shorts had blood on the front. This blood was later found to be consistent with that of the victim. Among the personal effects seized from defendant was a small photograph of April Sweet.[1]

Through an interpreter, Zuniga waived any objections to extradition and was immediately transported back to North Carolina. Upon arrival in Alexander County, he was charged with first-degree murder and rape.

In February 1985, Zuniga was tried and convicted of both charges and received the death penalty for the murder, as well as a sentence of life imprisonment for the rape. However, the death sentence was later vacated, after his attorneys successfully argued that the Mexican national suffered from "mild to moderate mental retardation, with an intellectual age of seven," and was not capable of understanding his heinous crime.[2]

The North Carolina State Supreme Court effectively commuted Zuniga's death sentence to life imprisonment.[3]

During the lengthy appeals process, which lasted over 15 years, psychologist Dr. Antonio Puente testified for the defense that Zuniga was in possession of 56 IQ. Another psychologist later testified that Zuniga scored a 64 on an IQ test he administered.[4]

In short, Zuniga will not be put to death but will spend the rest of his life behind bars, being financially supported by the taxpayers of North Carolina.

Today, the child killer resides among the general population in North Carolina's Central Prison in Raleigh. Since entering prison on Feb. 19, 1985, Zuniga has committed more than a dozen infractions, including "theft" and "self injury."[5]

In May 2017, Zuniga, otherwise known as prisoner #0458590, will turn 61 years old. He currently resides in a facility which has a fully functioning hospital, complete with operating room and x-ray labs.

8

Kristopher William Eggle

Age: 28
Location of Death: Organ Pipe Cactus National Monument Park, Arizona
Killer(s): Mexican Drug Cartel Members

On August 9, 2002, Ranger Eggle was killed by Mexican drug dealers while on duty in Arizona's Organ Pipe Cactus National Monument Park. Eggle was attempting to apprehend two smugglers, after being notified by Mexican authorities that the two had crossed the border and were headed into the park.

One of the drug dealers opened fire on Ranger Eggle with an AK-47. He was apparently struck below his protective vest, inflicting what would be a mortal wound. He died before a medevac helicopter arrived on the scene. Mexican police officers shot and killed Eggle's murderer.[1]

U.S. Park Ranger Eggle, 28, left behind his grieving parents and his sister (also a U.S. Park Ranger).

Kris's mom, Bonnie Eggle, sat down for the following interview about her brave son:

Q: *Where were you and how did you find out your son had been killed?*

A: I was visiting my daughter who was working at Yellowstone National Park that summer. We had been out touring in the a.m. and came home for lunch around oneish. Shortly after we arrived, there was a knock at the door. Jen went to answer and it was another Ranger named Mike—she invited him in and was chit-chatting with him. I thought he acted very nervous. He asked Jennifer to sit down. And then he blurted out the words, "Kris was been shot and he is in very bad shape!" (We found out later he knew Kris was dead, but Bob wanted to call us and tell us.) We kept saying we needed to go to him and NOW. We were both crying and kept asking where was he shot? He didn't answer us. I just kept saying he needs us—let's go.

All of a sudden there were 4 more Rangers in Jen's house, including the Chief Ranger, and the phone rang. It was Bob. He was at home in Cadillac and was notified by the Cadillac Sheriff's Department and then the NPS Superintendent from Organ Pipe Cactus National Monument. He told everyone, no one was to tell Jen or me. He needed to do that.

Jen answered the phone and kept saying, "No, Dad, no! No, Dad, no!" Then she handed me the phone and I was screaming "NO. NO. NO. I need to get to him. He needs me." Bob kept saying, "Bonnie, you can't go to him now. He is dead and they have taken his body to Phoenix for an autopsy." I did not want to believe it and kept saying. ...No. No. No. I just remember standing up and falling and one of he Rangers catching me before I hit the floor. I was screaming and sobbing and couldn't stop. It just could not be true.

The Chief Ranger told us to go pack our bags and they were making arrangements to take us to an airport in Montana that could get us out to Phoenix in the a.m. Both Jennifer and I did that, but I could hardly focus. She kept encouraging me to keep packing so we could leave.

U.S. Park Ranger Kris Eggle, 28, was shot and killed in the line of duty at Organ Pipe Cactus National Monument on August 9, 2002. The Kris Eggle Visitor Center (left), Kris Eggle at Canyonlands National Park (top), Kris and the Eggle family at Christmas.

I thought we should be able to get to Phoenix that night, but there were no flights from any of the little airports until the next a.m.

The Rangers took us to Bozeman, Montana, where they got us a motel and made arrangements for a flight at 6 a.m. The motel lined up a driver to take us. Jennifer and I just laid in bed, wrapped in each others' arms and sobbed all night. If there was any sleep, it was very little. Just plain horrible.

We arrived at the airport and the rest of this nightmare was to unfold....

Q: *How has your life changed since this tragedy?*

A: Our lives have been forever changed since Kris was murdered on August 9, 2002. Our hearts were totally shattered and still are....but we have picked up the pieces and tried to move forward with our daily lives. That is one reason why we as a family decided to get involved with writing letters to Congress members, doing interviews on television and radio, and going to different conferences where we spoke about what had happened and how Kris' death impacted us and hundreds of others, making appointments with members of the Senate and House and meeting with them (including J.D. Hayworth, Peter Hoekstra, Tom Tancredo, Dave Camp, Steve King).

We tried to get meetings with John McCain and Carl Levin and John Cornyn but could not make it work to meet. We also spent lots of time with DOI and National Park Service people to insist on proper border security to keep the illegals out and protect the American citizens. My husband has spoken before a Congressional hearing on funding of the border wall to cut down on the flow of illegals.

They, also at that time, talked about getting e-verify in place. We also had several meetings in our local area, but also traveled to many different states to speak about Kris, show videos of him and of his murder site. Numbers USA and FAIR were also organizations we kept closely in touch with. (We were given lots of promises, some ideas actually have happened, but not many.)

We still do some lobbying in the way we can, but not like we did for the first six to eight years after Kris was murdered.

Someone once said to me, things really don't move along as well *unless* mothers get involved—just like Mothers Against Drunk Driving (MADD)...I think I believe this is true. I was the one who kept us involved by talking to radio and television agents to set up interviews, contacting newspapers and websites to write articles, getting friends, neighbors, and family to write to every member of Congress, which some did three or four different times. Only a few answered back.

Keeping so busy helped us stay focused on helping the people on the ground in the different agencies. This is what we know Kris would have wanted us to do. We were speaking for him and hoping he would be proud of what we were trying to accomplish.

We miss Kris every day. We have gone 15 Christmases, 15 birthdays, 15 Mothers' Days and Fathers' Days, and all other holidays without him.

Our grief counselor told us to start making different traditions and not do things the same way because it would be too torturous, so we did change our Christmas tradition. Our hearts remain "hollow, empty, and shattered," but we try to put on "happy faces" to move through life. *But it is so tough* without our precious Kristopher William Eggle, and life will never be the same. I will never see him get married or have children. We have been robbed of those special parts of lives. We will never see him again until we are reunited in Heaven. That is what I hold onto—each day that goes by brings us one day closer to Kris.

During this past election, it was difficult to keep some of the friendships we had because we were for strong borders and national security, protection of our law enforcement agents/officers throughout our country. But, we had to be honest and say how we felt and that their candidate was an insider with many troubling things from her past. They did not want to listen to any of it. She is so evil and destructive, it's hard to see how anyone could not see through her facade. Trump was not our first choice, but he ended up as the only choice. I believe he was and still is serious about protecting America, our borders, and all of the men and women who enforce our laws on the front lines.

Q: *How was the issue that the killer was here illegally covered by the local media?*

A: Some media did not want to call Kris's killer and his accomplice illegal alien drug smugglers, but we insisted when we talked to people that they were that exactly. The killer entered the U.S. illegally (running from Mexican law and some cartel members) and came into Organ Pipe to get away from those chasing them. Kris was the backup to the Border Patrol and he was such a fast runner they had him chase on the ground as he was given directions from the Black Hawk helicopter flying above.

Our local media did an amazing job of covering Kris's death, but being in northern Michigan, not a lot of people had heard or understood about the illegal invasion. More are very aware of it now because of our family and friends continuing to talk about it and sharing about how it has affected thousands and thousands across this country.

The media, including television, radio, newspapers, etc., had a difficult time using those words. Whenever we spoke, we corrected them by using the proper and exact terms. They called them illegal immigrants...*outrageous*! Our local news provided good coverage for a length of time and we were happy about that. Even some other media in the USA would call us on anniversaries of his birthday or death and we would tell the story again and call these evil men exactly what they were. One of his killers is dead, the other who did not pull the trigger served his time—12 1/2 years and has been deported back to Mexico. He still has a life, can be married, have children, and live to be an old man....but not our KRIS.

Q: *What kind of person was Kris? What were his goals, dreams, etc.?*

A: Kris was an amazing young man. He was trustworthy, kind, caring, loving, and a strong person of faith. As a little boy, he showed those characteristics and continued right through the rest of his life. He was a beautiful runner, winning many awards in cross country and track events. He was valedictorian of his high school class and graduated from the University of Michigan. He intended to become a doctor, but that changed for him when I was diagnosed with cancer.

I had my surgery and treatments there at the University of Michigan Hospital and he spent lots of time with me during those weeks and months. After that, he got his cross country team to do volunteer work at the Children's Hospital and Kris himself volunteered at the hospital doing various tasks, including writing letters for patients, reading books to them, praying with them, and visiting those who needed someone to care. Because of him spending so much time doing this, he realized he did not want to spend his work days inside of a building; therefore, he decided to move into the Outdoor Science field, and in turn, he also chose then to pursue law enforcement as well.

Dedication of the Kris Eggle Visitor Center, Organ Pipe Cactus National Monument, July 29, 2003.

He explored many different agencies that offered these options and chose the Department of the Interior and National Park Service, where his "dreams" could be fulfilled. He loved what he was doing, and being able to travel our country and spend time in our beautiful national parks and monuments. When he took a law enforcement position at Organ Pipe National Monument, he knew it was different than any of the other challenges he had faced in his jobs. The illegal invasion was awful, including drugs and weapons flowing almost nonstop. He told us he wanted to make a difference to try and keep these evils out of our country in order to help protect American citizens, and especially children. He and his Ranger partners did this (and still do) until the day he was murdered. And, that is when we lost part of our family, part of our hearts—forever loved; forever missed.

Q: *What would you like the public to know about this tragedy?*

A: All members of our family want people to understand that our son's murder did not have to happen and could have been avoided, but because our government did *not* stand firm (even 15 years ago) about secure borders and the illegal invasion, we were denied spending the rest of our lives with our precious son Kris. I am so thankful for the many, many organizations, and other families who are now standing up and standing firm against the travesties done against them as well. Promises from Congress are weak and fickle and that has been proven time and time again. But we must persevere and stand strong to hold their "feet to the fire." We also were thankful for President Trump's declaration of building a "border wall" and clamping down on this invasion and the lawbreakers. Let's pray that his pledges will be fulfilled.

9

Richard V. Grossi

Age: 55
Location of Death: Worcester, Massachussetts
Killer: Maria Tavares Leite

On October 21, 2009, Richard Grossi died at the University of Massachusetts Medical Center in Worcester as a result of the catastrophic injuries he received a few weeks earlier when Maria Leite, an unlicensed illegal alien, slammed her car into Grossi in Milford.

On September 12, 2009, Leite failed to yield on Fruit Street Extension, and cut across South Main Street onto Fruit Street. She then crashed her 1998 Kia SUV into the 2002 Dodge sedan Grossi was driving south on South Main, according to police.

Leite was originally arraigned on charges of unlicensed driving and failure to stop or yield, but after Grossi passed away, the charge of motor vehicle homicide by negligent driving was brought against her.

She came to this country from Portugal on a 90-day travel visa, and overstayed by four years.

However, before she stood trial for the more serious charges, she was deported back to her native Portugal on July 29, 2010.

On August 6, 2010, *The Telegram & Gazette* reported:

> After hearing from Mr. Rubin, Judge Andrew D'Angelo issued a default warrant for Mrs. Leite on the motor vehicle homicide charge, which means she would be subject to arrest if she returns from Portugal.
>
> Mrs. Leite pleaded guilty July 2 in a packed courtroom in Milford District Court during an hour-long session in which several members of Mr. Grossi's family gave victim-

impact statements, telling Judge D'Angelo how devastated they were by Mr. Grossi's death.

Judge D'Angelo sentenced Mrs. Leite on July 2 to two years in the House of Correction with six months to serve. However, after consulting with her lawyer, Paulo J. Moura of Plymouth, she decided to withdraw her guilty plea. Mr. Moura was not at this morning's hearing, which lasted less than a minute....

After today's court appearance, Mr. Grossi's sister, Maureen Grossi Laquerre of Bellingham, said the family wasn't surprised by what happened in court.

"This is what she wanted from the very beginning. I predicted this from the beginning," she said of Mrs. Leite.

"The federal government needs to step up with the enforcement of the laws that are in place," she said. "The illegals have no regard for our laws. They are killing people left and right and getting away with it. It's a disgrace."[1]

Grossi's obituary reported the following details about the life, of which he was robbed:

Mr. Grossi was employed by the Benjamin Moore Co.

> in Milford for 27 years. He was born May 22, 1954 in Providence, Rhode Island, son of the late Vincent R. and Veronica (Riley) Grossi. He attended Milford High School. In his spare time, Richard enjoyed spending time with family and friends. He loved children, especially his Godchild and grand nieces. Richard loved to fish, spending as much time as possible at the ocean and Cape Cod was his favorite place to be. He was an avid animal lover and a kind and loving person to all who knew him.[2]

Richard's sister, Kathleen DiBari, shared her experience over this tragedy:

Q: *Where were you and how did you find out your brother had been killed?*

A: I was at home when I got a call that he had been in a serious accident. I rushed to hospital and was told that he wasn't good at all and to be prepared for the worst. I did get to see him surrounded by nurses, doctors, paramedics, and police and before I even realized what was happening, he was being transported to another hospital—not by plane because I guess the day was too overcast to fly, but by ambulance.

There was no time to think. I called my sister and picked up his girlfriend on the way to the hospital, only to wait for hours before they actually found us, waiting in the emergency room.

Q: *How has your life changed since this tragedy?*

A: I had nightmares about him having surgery for so long, and really too there's too much to explain all the problems related to the crash. I lost a brother and a great fun-loving friend. I was in shock when he passed away six and a half weeks later, as he "came to" for a short while, only to slide back into the final coma of his life. It took the spark out of my life for a long time.

Q: *How was the issue that the killer was here illegally covered by the local media?*

A: The local media gave little to no coverage on the accident until his death, weeks later.The fact that the police on scene drove the "other illegal" home from the accident still blows my mind as well as being treated by the one police person "in charge" of the accident scene couldn't even give me the time of day when I went to see him at the station trying to glean as much information about my brother's accident. There's always a "bad apple" that keeps being carried until retirement vs. a few others who gave condolences and told me he was a "good guy," and he sure was to us!

Q: *What kind of person was Richard? What were his goals, dreams, etc.?*

A: I would like to think that Richard was just beginning his life over again and the possibilities ahead were great. He had worked at Benjamin Moore Paint for too many years for me to remember, and was recently laid off before his passing. He was planning a trip to Florida with a friend and he had plans to open an ILOPS shop, which stands for "I Love Other People's Stuff." He loved getting hand-me-downs from us four sisters, only to be given away to someone who was in need. He was the type of person who'd give you the shirt from his back.

Q: *What would you like the public to know about this tragedy?*

A: I hope all of this information is useful and can possibly help someone else, because I've had to stop, remember, and put into words this very difficult "thing" that happened to ordinary people living in a town that we were brought up and facing a loss that we remember in different but similar light eight years later.

10

Maxey Ann Lynch

Age: 61
Location of Death: Mecklenburg County, Virginia
Killer: Santos Gabriel-Tomas

On October 25, 2013, Mecklenburg County Circuit Judge Leslie M. Osborn sentenced Santos Gabriel-Tomas, 30, to 10 years behind bars for killing 61-year-old Maxey Ann Lynch, earlier this year.

Two months earlier, Gabriel-Tomas pleaded guilty to aggravated DUI manslaughter, DUI second offense, and driving without an operator's license.

Gabriel-Tomas speaks only Spanish and required the use of an interpreter throughout his court proceedings.

In the early morning hours of April 7, Gabriel-Tomas crashed into a 1999 Ford Escort driven by Lynch, who was a newspaper carrier for *The Richmond Times-Dispatch*.

The Guatemalan national was driving in the wrong direction on U.S. 58 and had a blood alcohol concentration (BAC) of 0.19 percent at the time of the wreck, which is more than twice the state's legal limit.

Lynch was airlifted to Virginia Commonwealth University Medical Center, where she was later pronounced dead.

At sentencing, Mecklenburg Deputy Commonwealth's Attorney Allen Nash, told Judge Osborn: "He [Gabriel-Tomas] said he had been drinking beer and liquor with friends and that he doesn't remember going home."

Incredibly, it was actually the illegal alien's second DUI conviction in less than two years.

The Richmond Times-Dispatch reported:

> Tomas had never acquired a license to drive, and after he was convicted in March 2012 of his first drunken driving offense in Lunenburg County, a judge revoked his privileges to obtain a license for 12 months as part of his punishment.
>
> After the suspension period passed, Tomas continued to drive without a license and was doing so when he killed Lynch.[1]

In April 2012, *The New York Times* reported that the U.S. Immigration and Customs Enforcement Agency (ICE), under Obama, would no longer issue ICE holds on illegal aliens who had only been charged with traffic violations.[2]

For years, the now-retired Rep. Sue Myrick (R-NC) tried and failed to get the so-called Scott Gardner Act through Congress. This measure would have required the immediate deportation of any illegal alien convicted of drinking and driving.[3]

Such a measure may have saved the life of Mrs. Lynch.

Maxey Lynch left behind her husband of 19 years, two sons, a stepdaughter and six grandchildren.

One person left the following remembrance in Mrs. Lynch's online obituary:

> Our deepest sympathies to Levi and the family. Maxey will be greatly and sadly missed. She was a wonderful lady. She was a wife, grandmother, friend, sister, cousin who wanted everyone around her to hear her laughter. Will miss your laugh my friend. [4]

11

Bob Clark

Age: 67
Location of Death: Pacific Coast Highway
Killer: Hector Velazquez-Nava

Though the 1983 movie *A Christmas Story* did not make much of an impression when it was initially released, it has since become a perennial holiday favorite with families across the country. We are not only treated to Ralphie's hilarious quest to obtain a Red Ryder BB gun, but the film also reminds us, at least a little, of our own childhood Christmases past.

While most of us are familiar with the cult classic, many may not know the tragic way in which the director of *A Christmas Story*, Bob Clark, died. He was killed by a drunk-driving illegal alien.

On April 4, 2007, as the 67-year-old director was traveling along the Pacific Coast Highway with his son, Ariel Hanrath-Clark, 22, when an SUV veered into oncoming traffic, causing a head-on collision with Clark's vehicle. Both father and son died at the scene.[1]

The driver of that SUV was Hector Velazquez-Nava, a previously deported Mexican national living in Los Angeles. He had 0.24 blood-alcohol concentration (BAC)—three times the state's legal limit.

The illegal alien had no driver's license and had a 2004 conviction for solicitation of a prostitute in Los Angeles. For that conviction, Velazquez-Nava was sentenced to 24 months' probation and a $1,500 fine.

On October 16, 2007, Hector Velazquez-Nava was sentenced to six years in prison after pleading no contest on two counts of gross vehicular manslaughter while intoxicated.[2]

As you and yours continue to enjoy *A Christmas Story* over the coming years, take a moment to remember the man who brought you that movie and his broken family.

12

Mirjana Puhar

Age: 19

Location of Death: Charlotte, North Carolina

Killers: Edward Sanchez and Emmanuel Jesus Rangel

On February 24, 2015, Charlotte-Mecklenburg County police discovered three dead bodies at a home in the 700 block of Norris Drive. All had been shot to death.

One the victims was 19-year-old Mirjana Puhar, a finalist on the popular show, "America's Next Top Model."[1]

The bodies of 23-year-old Jonathan Cosme Alvarado, and 22-year-old Jusmar Isaiah Gonzaga-Garcia were also found in the residence.

Police determined the shootings were drug-related.

Both Edward Sanchez and Emmanuel Rangel were charged with multiple counts of first-degree murder, and booked into the Mecklenburg County Jail on Immigration and Customs Enforcement (ICE) detainers.

As it turns out, Rangel was also wanted for the recent murder of 22-year-old Rosool Jaleel Harrell, who was shot to death inside a car in Matthews, North Carolina.

Puhar came to this country from Serbia with her family when she was only five years old. In her teen years, she worked at a McDonald's while struggling to make it as a model.

Ironically, shortly before her death, Puhar posted a message on Instagram, stating: "I have a dream that one day we will one day spread more love than we do hate," reported WBTV.[2]

In April 2017, Sanchez was convicted on four counts of first-degree murder.

The Charlotte Observer reported:

> After a 10-day trial, Sanchez, 21, received a life sentence without parole for each death, plus another 13 years for a separate attempted murder conviction. One of his victims was Mirjana Puhar, a former contestant on the TV show, "America's Next Top Model."
>
> The killings occurred in February 2015: Rosool Harrell, 22, a Xanax dealer, was shot three times in the back outside a Matthews hotel. A companion of Harrell's was seriously wounded.
>
> Puhar, 19, her heroin-dealer boyfriend Jonathan "Cupie" Alvarado, 23, and Jusmar Gonzaga-Garcia, 21, were found shot to death two days later in a small house not far from uptown.
>
> After deliberating for about 90 minutes, the jury announced its verdict to Superior Court Judge Eric Levinson around midday.[3]

Rangel is still awaiting trial for the same murder spree which took the life of the 19-year-old model.

It should be noted that while NBC News, Access Hollywood, *The New York Daily News*, and *The Washington Post*, among others, all reported on Puhar's murder, not one of them mentioned the fact that her accused killers are in the country illegally.

13

Matthew Denice

Age: 23
Location of Death: Milford, Massachussetts
Killer: Nicolas Guaman

On August 20, 2011, Milford police arrested Nicholas Dutan Guaman, 34, after he struck a man riding his motorcycle.

The victim, Matthew Denice, was hit and dragged close to a quarter of a mile by the pickup truck Guaman was driving, according to Milford Police Chief Thomas O'Loughlin.

Numerous witnesses said they tried to stop Guaman as he continued to drag the young man through the streets of Milford.

On August 22, 2011, *The Boston Globe* reported:

> "I've seen a lot of things in 30 years, and this is right up there," said Milford Police Chief Thomas O'Loughlin in a phone interview. "He dragged the guy for a quarter-mile. He was alive for a good portion of it."
>
> Samuel Schwenninger, 37, who lives on West Street, was among the frantic witnesses who gave chase, trying to make the driver stop. But he did not.
>
> The driver "just kind of stared at us blankly," Schwenninger said. "I could see [Denice] grimacing through the viser on his helmet. I won't soon forget that."
>
> Finally, at the corner of West Street and Bancroft Avenue, police say, Guaman left the road. Gouges in a sloping lawn were still fresh yesterday, and spray paint circled dark stains on the sidewalk where Denice dislodged from the truck and where witnesses found him dead.[1]

> Chief O'Loughlin told reporters that Guaman was in the country illegally from Ecuador.
>
> Guaman was charged with second-degree murder, DUI, negligent operation, leaving the scene of personal injury and death, possession of an open container of alcohol in a vehicle, failure to stop for police, driving without a license, failure to stop or yield, resisting arrest, and wanton or reckless conduct creating risk to a child.
>
> In May 2014, Worcester Superior Court Judge David Ricciardone found Guaman guilty of manslaughter by motor vehicle and motor vehicle homicide while driving under the influence of alcohol.
>
> Guaman was sentenced to 12 to 14 years in prison.
>
> Matthew "graduated with honors and was awarded 'most dependable' from Milford High School, class of 2006," according to his obituary.[2]

Matthew's mom, Maureen Maloney, shared the following thoughts on this tragic loss:

Q: *Where were you and how did you find out your son had been killed?*
A: I was home when I received the call that my son, Matthew, had been in an accident and I that should come to the hospital. My blood immediately ran cold as terror overcame me. The hospital is three miles from our home and on the way, we passed Matthew's motorcycle laying in the road. There didn't appear to be any damage to the motorcycle and I actually breathed a sigh of relief thinking maybe he wasn't hurt too bad.

Once I arrived at the emergency room and I was put in the little waiting room, I knew the news was going to be horrific. It seemed like an eternity waiting for the doctor to come speak with us. I begged the nurse to please tell me what was going on but she couldn't. The doctor finally came in, and in a matter of fact tone—informed us that they had tried to save Matthew but they couldn't and that he had died.

He was dead when he arrived at the hospital and they could not resuscitate him. Then I heard the most primal, guttural noise I have ever heard as my husband started screaming and punching the furniture. I went into a state of shock. The hours that followed while we waited to see Matthew's body are a blur and I still get numb thinking about it.

Q: *How has your life changed since this tragedy?*
A: Since Matthew's death everything in my life has changed. In the initial days, weeks and months, the simplest tasks like brushing my

teeth or taking a shower, seemed foreign like I was learning how to do things all over again. I equate it to recovering from a debilitating illness. I thought for sure I was going to die from a broken heart. In my line of work, I have seen patients with Takotsubo or "broken heart syndrome" and I still can't believe I did not succumb to it.

My life is divided between before Matthew's death and after. I have had my last "happiest day of my life," for without Matthew there can never be a happiest day of my life. My last happiest day was May 21, 2011, when Matthew graduated from college. He was my first child to graduate college and I was so proud of him. I had my other son and husband beside me, our family was all together.

There is nothing like the pain and trauma of losing a child. A part of me died with Matthew. My heart is split between the present with my surviving son and heaven with Matthew. Sadly, many people don't know how to deal with a parent's inconsolable heartbreak. It leaves people feeling helpless so they avoid us or avoid talking about Matthew. I've lost friends and had family members distance themselves, but I have also gained some of the most wonderful friends. The sun still rises each morning, it's just not as bright as it used to be. However, at night the stars seem brighter knowing Matthew is in heaven looking down on us.

As the shock wore off, I realized Matthew's death was completely preventable. My son should still be alive. The illegal alien that killed him should never have been in the country. I, who am normally a quiet person who doesn't like attention, became an outspoken advocate against illegal immigration. I will use the huge void left by Matthew's absence to speak out and try to prevent other innocent citizens from being killed.

Q: *How was the issue that the killer was here illegally covered by the local media?*

A: Matthew was the third person to be killed by an illegal alien in a two-year period in our town. Appallingly, when the first two victims, Richard Grossi and Andrea Agosta, were killed, their stories barely made the police blotter.

People were outraged that an illegal alien, who should have never been in the country, killed Matthew in such a horrific, barbaric manner. Therefore, the local media gave a significant amount of coverage to the tragedy and the fact that his killer was an illegal alien. Matthew's tragedy also captured national media attention. It has been six years and the local media still contacts me for interviews when illegal immigration issues are in the news.

Americans are being killed and maimed every day by illegal aliens and it is an atrocity that the media is not covering the stories.

Q: *What kind of person was Matthew? What were his goals, dreams, etc.?*

A: Matthew was more than I could ever have hoped for in a son. He was kind, caring, outgoing, and one of the happiest and funniest people I have ever known. He always had a smile on his face and had a genuine love for people. When he walked into a room his smile and personality made others smile and the room lit up. He was happy, full of life, selfless, a good American young man with good American values. Everybody in our home town of Milford knew Matthew, if not personally, they knew him because he always had a kind word, a smile, thumbs up or peace sign as he went by.

Matthew graduated college with a dual degree in Information Technology and Business three months prior to his death. He had taken the police academy examination and planned on being a police officer working in cyber crime. Two weeks prior to his death he started his first professional job in Information Technology.

Matthew had so many goals, dreams, and passions. He had a long-term girlfriend that he planned on marrying. He loved children and wanted a large family. He dreamed of buying a house. He would jokingly tell me he was going to buy the house across the street from us so I could watch his kids. One of Matthew's short-term goals was to drive across the country helping a friend move to California. He loved skateboarding, snowboarding, working on cars, fishing, paint balling, sports, and his Subaru club. He was an avid fan of the Boston sports teams.

Q: *What would you like the public to know about this tragedy?*

A: Matthew's death was totally preventable. If our immigration laws had been enforced, my son's killer would have been deported years before he killed my son. My son wasn't killed in the initial collision. Medical experts and witnesses testified in the trial that Matthew survived the collision with contusions and abrasions. If the illegal alien had not fled, Matthew would still be alive.

Matthew was killed when the illegal alien driver fled the scene and ran Matthew over, causing him to become lodged under the truck.

Then, he dragged Matthew a quarter of a mile to his death. Witnesses were banging on the truck trying to get the driver to stop; if he had stopped perhaps Matthew could have survived his injuries. Matthew was dislodged from the truck after the illegal alien ran off the road. Then he backed up over Matthew and continued to flee. Matthew's injuries included a punctured heart, punctured lungs, a torn aorta, all of his ribs were fractured in multiple places, his intestines were eviscerated and spilled out onto the sidewalk, and the flesh and muscle were torn from his arms, legs, and stomach.

Matthew's death has affected many people. It's not just about the person that is killed. My husband I have lost our son, future daughter-in-law, and future grandchildren. Matthew's girlfriend has lost her future husband, children, and the life they planned to have. My other son lost his brother and now he is an only child. Matthew's cousins all miss him dearly and the younger ones couldn't understand why Matthew was gone. All of Matthew's friends have lost their friend.

Many of the witnesses and first-responders were traumatized by Matthews death and required counseling. The ripple effects of his death spread far and wide as it does with most deaths.

Each day 20 Americans are killed by illegal aliens, that's 7,300 Americans killed each year, and all of these deaths were and are preventable. None of us are immune to this epidemic. We need Americans to demand our current laws be enforced and illegal aliens deported.

14

Officer Daryl Raetz

Age: 29
Location of Death: Phoenix, Arizona
Killer: Jesus Molina

On September 26, 2014, Jesus Cabrera Molina, 25, who killed a Phoenix police officer in 2013, was sentenced by Maricopa County Judge David Gass to eight years in prison. The Mexican national pleaded guilty to negligent homicide and hit-and-run with death or injury.

On May 19, 2013, the victim, Officer Daryl Raetz was conducting a traffic stop at the intersection of 51st Street and Cambridge Avenue when he was struck by an SUV driven by Molina. The officer was left lying in road, as Molina fled the scene.

Officer Daryl Raetz was later pronounced dead at a local hospital.

Molina admitted that he had been drinking and snorting cocaine only hours before the fatal crash, according to police.

Fox 10 reported that the officer's widow, Stephanie Raetz, made the following statement after Molina as sentenced:

> It also helps me to know I looked him in the eyes and told him how I felt and that's something that he has to live with for the rest of his life and he has to live with the fact that he killed my husband, her son, his brother.. for the rest of his life… I don't believe he is remorseful at all… He still has yet to admit that he did anything wrong and is guilty, so I don't feel like he has any remorse whatsoever.[1]

In addition to his wife, Officer Daryl Raetz left behind a wife and a 7-year-old daughter. He had served with the Phoenix Police Department since 2007, and was a veteran of the Iraq War.[2]

Molina, who has a previous history of DUIs, was deported in 2011. However, the illegal alien was able to make his way back to Phoenix with little difficulty, and was actually arrested again in 2012 and turned over to Immigration and Customs Enforcement (ICE) officials, who released him despite his previous criminal history.

In May 2013, ICE released the following statement:

> In March 2012, ICE placed Mr. Cabrera-Molina in removal proceedings and detained him following his incarceration in the Maricopa County Jail on a charge unrelated to this most recent arrest. Mr. Cabrera-Molina was ordered released from ICE custody in May 2012 after he posted the $5,000 bond granted by an immigration judge with the Department of Justice's Executive Office of Immigration Review. His removal proceedings remain pending at this time.[3]

Officer Raetz is only one one of several Phoenix police officers who have been killed by an illegal alien in recent years.

15

Sister Denise Mosier

Age: 66
Location of Death: Prince William County, Virginia
Killer: Carlos A. Martinelly Montano

On August 1, 2010, Prince William County police arrested Carlos A. Martinelly Montano, 24, after he slammed head on into a car in which three Benedictine nuns were traveling. While Sister Denise Mosier was killed instantly, her two companions were taken by helicopter to the hospital with serious injuries.

Sister Charlotte Lange had a metal plate inserted into her right leg, and Sister Connie Ruth Lupton spent four months in the hospital, with 14 broken bones.

As a result of the case, the Virginia Department of Motor Vehicles no longer accepts federal work authorization cards as proof of legal residence, which is how Martinelly Montano obtained a driver's license even though he was in the middle of deportation proceedings.

Also, in August 2011, Prince William County sued the Department of Homeland Security in an effort to discover what action (if any) the federal agency had taken against the more than 3,000 illegal aliens the county had turned over to Immigration and Customs Enforcement (ICE) for deportation.

The measure was taken after Prince William County police began noticing that the illegal aliens they arrested for various crimes, and then turned over to ICE, kept showing up in their jail.

What follows is a list of a few of Montano's offenses:

• April 2009...he was arrested for driving without a license and convicted in June.

• October 2008...he was stopped for driving 55 in a 35 mph zone, and had a .17 BAC (blood alcohol concentration) level. Montano was sentenced to three years probation and his driver's license was suspended.

• December 2007...he was arrested for being drunk in public.

• July 2007...he was charged with DUI and convicted later that same year.[1]

Though ICE ordered Montano to be deported in March 2009, he continued to have run-ins with the law and remained free.

According to spokesman Jonathan Perok, Prince William County Police notified ICE after both his first and second DUI arrests.

In 2010, Corey Stewart, chairman of the Prince William Board of Supervisors, issued the following statement on the case:

> The despicable thing is that this criminal was...handed over to ICE twice, and released by ICE twice. He's gone out and killed a nun. That's a perfect example of what's wrong with immigration enforcement in this country. The blame is on representatives in Congress for being so flaccid on the issue, and they continue not to fund the deportation of illegal immigrants in this country.

In an ironic twist of fate, at the time of the fatal wreck, Montano was actually being defended by Hogar Immigrant Services, a division of Catholic Charities in the Arlington Diocese.

In February 2011, the Prince William Board of County Supervisors issued a statement on the federal government's responsibility for Mosier's death. A portion of that statement follows:

> The County learned in August 2010 that Carlos Martinelly Montano—who is currently charged with felony murder, involuntary manslaughter, and drunken driving in the death of Sister Denise Mosier—was released into the community by ICE officials knowing he was in the country illegally. This prompted the Prince William Board of County Supervisors (BOCS) to submit a Freedom of Information Act (FOIA) request into the actions by the Department of Homeland Security and ICE that led to Montano's release. It also sparked questions and a separate FOIA request regarding what ICE has done with the

> more than 3,000 criminal illegal aliens that Prince William County turned over to ICE through the 287(g) program.
>
> "The Department of Homeland Security has an obligation to the citizens of Prince William County to explain what they are doing to uphold their obligation to help make our communities safe from criminals like Montano and the other 3,000 criminals we have turned over to ICE," said BOCS Chairman Corey Stewart. "Clearly they made major mistakes in the Montano case and don't want to be held accountable to the public for those, but we need to know how deep these problems run. Was the Montano case an anomaly, or is this business as usual for ICE? When we turn these criminals over to ICE, it is with the expectation that they are going to do something about these criminals in our community."[2]

In February 2012, Prince William County Circuit Court Judge Lon Farris sentenced Martinelly Montano to 20 years in prison for the murder of Sister Denise, as well as for a host of other charges. The Bolivian national could have received up to 70 years behind bars.

16

Darness Brown

Age: 10
Location of Death: Boynton Beach, Florida
Killer: Leticia Flores

On December 7, 2009, Boynton Beach police arrested Leticia Flores, 28, for the hit-and-run killing of 10-year-old Darness Brown. The girl's 13-year-old sister, Darneisha Ellis, was also injured when Flores allegedly hit their scooter.

Boynton Beach police spokeswoman Stephanie Slater said the girls were riding their scooter on Southwest Ninth Avenue at Southwest Third Street when Flores hit them with her Honda SUV.

In what had to be a sickening scene, Darneisha told the police that as her sister was dying next to her, Flores jumped out of her vehicle and screamed at the two girls for being on the street; she then fled the scene.

The girl's story was supported by an eyewitness. Jessica Thomas, 24, told police she ran outside when she heard the crash. The affidavit claims: "Once outside, she observed the driver of the vehicle standing outside staring at the injured pedestrian. Thomas then stated that the driver (Flores) got into her vehicle and fled the scene."[1]

Police caught up to Flores as she pulled into a convenience store parking lot. She told the arresting officers that she left the accident scene because there were other people who had come to the girls' aid. She also said that she ran because she had no driver's license.

A good Samaritan performed CPR on the little girl until paramedics arrived. However, having sustained severe internal damage, she died shortly after arriving at Delray Medical Center.

17

Deputy Josie Fox

Age: 37
Location of Death: Millard County, Utah
Killer: Roberto Miramontes Roman

On January 5, 2010, Deputy Josie Fox pulled over the 1995 Cadillac Deville being driven by Roberto Miramontes Roman on U.S. Highway 50. Detectives say that during the stop, Ramon shot Fox slightly above her bullet-proof vest.

The following day, acting on a tip from a homeowner, sheriff's deputies in Beaver County, Utah, burst into a shed where Mexican nationals Roberto Miramontes Roman and Ruben Chavez Reyes (the passenger) were sleeping, and took both men into custody without incident.

Among other offenses, Roman had been caught twice in the past for re-entering this country illegally, the last such arrest and prosecution coming in 2005.

According to Immigration and Customs Enforcement, Roman entered the country legally in 1990, but because of numerous criminal convictions, was deported in 1998. Roman is a convicted drug dealer. A witness cooperating with the investigation claims that he bought drugs from Roman a few hours before he murdered Deputy Fox.

In May 2017, U.S. Attorney General Jeff Sessions made the following statement on Deputy Fox's murder:

> Deputy Sheriff Fox sacrificed her life trying to keep our country safe, and we must never forget that. I am grateful to the investigators and prosecutors who brought her killer to justice no matter how long it took.

> This case also demonstrates that we must enforce the rule of law along our southwest border, and confront the scourge of drug trafficking. During this National Police Week, and every day of the year, we must continue to stand behind our brave law enforcement officers, who do a dangerous job day in and day out.[1]

In January 2017, Roman pleaded guilty in federal court to multiple firearms and immigration violations. Additionally, the illegal alien was charged on several other federal charges, including the intentional killing of a law enforcement officer.

On May 18, 2017, The Salt Lake Tribune reported on Deputy Fox's mother's impact statement before Roman was sentenced:

> On Thursday, Fox's mother, Cindy Greathouse, with husband Russ Greathouse at her side, said their daughter was a "kind and beautiful and strong woman" who always knew growing up that she wanted to be a police officer.[2]

He was found guilty and sentenced to life in prison, plus 80 years.

Deputy Josie Fox, 37, served with the Millard County Sheriff's Office for five years. She left behind a husband and two children.

18

Brandon Abrams

Age: 6
Location of Death: San Antonio, Texas
Killer: Luis Enrique Landin

On January 24, 2013, San Antonio police arrested Luis Enrique Landin after he drove into 6-year-old Brandon Abrams as he waited on the sidewalk for the ice cream truck's daily visit.

Landin's Ford Ranger pickup truck jumped the curb and struck the little boy as he sat on his bicycle in the 9300 block of Autumn Sunrise, according to police.

A witness, Jane Withers, saw the crash from her house and immediately ran to the boy.

The impact was so great that it knocked the little boy out of his shoes.

Withers told the *San Antonio Express-News*:

> I saw (Brandon) fly in the air and hit the ground. I've never seen anyone fly through the air so much.... He was doing the right thing, riding on the sidewalk.[1]

Abrams was taken by helicopter to University Hospital.

Unfortunately, the boy quickly succumbed to his injuries and was pronounced dead shortly after arriving at the hospital.

The boy's mother, Nadia Abrams, tearfully told WOAI:

> He always wanted to just be outside. He always wanted to play. We were working on homework. The ice cream truck went by. I just was going to let him out long enough to get some ice cream.

The day after he was killed, many people, including Abrams' own

Cub Scout Pack 352, attended a candlelight vigil at the scene of the fatal crash.

Landin was originally charged with intoxication manslaughter and driving without a license, but the charges were later changed to criminally negligent homicide.

The illegal alien admitted to texting while driving and had dropped his phone, reaching-down to retrieve it when he hit the little boy.

As a further insult to Brandon's parents, in May 2014, a grand jury failed to indict Landin, and he walked free. It is not known if Immigration and Customs Enforcement (ICE) deported him.

Withers told the *San Antonio Express-News* that she was not surprised by the dissappointing outcome:

> Even if the grand jury had allowed the district attorney's office to pursue the case, previous trials in Bexar County indicate a prison sentence would have been far from guaranteed.[2]

As a result of Brandon's death, his grandfather, Steven Abrams, became an outspoken critic of "distracted driving" and lobbied the Texas State Legislature to pass a law banning texting while driving.

In May 2015, the measure (House Bill 80) died when 13 state senators refused to bring the proposed bill to the senate floor for a vote.

Following the bitter defeat, Steven Abrams told NBC News 4:

> As far as I'm concerned, they are cowards and going forward they are basically accomplices to murder whoever gets killed on Texas highways or roads or sidewalks or crosswalks. Those 13 senators, based on the statistics of about 500 people a year, each one of them will cost 38.5 lives and I hope they can live with that.[3]

In addition to his parents and grandparents, Brandon left behind two sisters, Jasmine and Hailey.

19

Louise Sollowin

Age: 93
Location of Death: Omaha, Nebraska
Killer: Sergio Martinez-Perez

In July 2013, Douglas County prosecutors charged Sergio Martinez-Perez, 19, with first-degree murder, after 93-year-old rape victim Louise Sollowin died in an Omaha hospital.

A few days earlier, police in Omaha arrested Martinez-Perez after he beat and raped the elderly woman in her home. The woman was found bloodied, with several serious injuries.

Omaha.com reported:

> The woman's daughter, who also lives in the residence, called 911. Officers said they discovered Perez nude and on top of the woman in a bedroom that had blood on the "walls, floor, ceiling and bed." The prosecution said that Perez admitted to police that he beat and raped the victim "because he was angry at women after a night of drinking."[1]

Perez was found naked and passed out on top of the victim, according to police. The victim's cheekbones, nose, and several teeth were broken in the ordeal.

Martinez-Perez, who speaks only Spanish, was employed as a roofer, and had only been in the country for two months when he attacked Sollowin.

He claimed that he became angry after leaving a party where his sexual advances were rejected by multiple women, and "randomly" selected Sollowin as his victim.

Martinez-Perez was charged with first-degree sexual assault, first-degree assault, and burglary. He was booked into the Douglas County Correctional Center on an immigration detainer.

The Journal Star reported:

> Louise Sollowin grew up in Omaha's Little Italy community, where her family started Orsi's Bakery. Her husband, a World War II veteran, died about 30 years ago.[2]

Sollowin lived in the home where the fatal attack took place for 71 years.

On April 9, 2014, Martinez-Perez pleaded guilty to first-degree murder, and was subsequently sentenced to life in prison by Douglas County District Judge Timothy Burns. The plea deal spared the illegal alien from the death penalty.

However, before his sentencing, WOWT reported:

> Last August, Louise's son Joe said, "I hope he gets the electric chair. And I want to be there for that. I hope he gets a beating way before that. I don't think dying is enough."[3]

"It was beyond belief what she had to endure," Judge Burns told the Sollowin family.

20

Kendrick Owens

Age: 13
Location of Death: New Caney, Texas
Killer: Javier Correa

On March 8, 2010, Kendrick was walking home with a friend, after spending the night at his father's house, along the road in New Caney, when the 1998 Dodge Dakota driven by Javier Correa, 28, went off onto the shoulder of the road and struck the 13-year-old boy.

Correa sped away from the scene, and drove to his nearby home.

A tow truck driver, who saw him hit Owens, followed Correa and alerted police to his location. That driver, Aubrey LaBuff of LaBuff Towing, drove to FM 1485 and US 59 to look for the erratic driver.

The Montgomery County Police reporter stated:

> [H]e saw the suspect vehicle turn under the freeway and start north. He made a U-turn and started to follow it, at the same time calling Montgomery County Sheriff's Office to report it.
>
> What he saw next changed his life forever as it did with many others. The truck struck Kendrick Owens and then kept going. Fighting the urge to stop he saw others stopping so he decided to follow the truck and call his locations out to dispatchers.
>
> As he did this, Kendrick's friend flagged down help, who started assisting Kendrick.
>
> LaBuff followed the truck to 17293 Oak Grove Lane just a few miles up the road. When Javier Correa reached his

> house and got out of his pickup to go inside, LaBuff says he told Correa he struck a child and Correa denied it.[1]

A few minutes later, Texas Department of Public Safety Troopers arrived at Correa's residence and took him into custody.

ABC 13 News reported:

> "I detained him and brought him back," said DPS Trooper Justin Lopez. "He'd been admitting that he'd been drinking this morning.[2]

Kendrick was flown by Life Flight to Hermann Hospital in Houston, where his mother, Rhonda West, spent one hour with her unconcsious son, before he was pronounced dead.

Correa was charged with intoxication manslaughter and failure to stop and render aid. Shortly after the fatal crash, the illegal alien was shown to have a Blood Alcohol Concentration (BAC) of .29, more than three times the legal limit.

According to police, several drivers called 911 to report Correa's reckless driving shortly before he hit the Keefer Crossing Middle School student.

Court records show that Correa had a prior DWI conviction in 2005, as well as a previous conviction for assault causing bodily injury in 2000.

In late December 2010, Correa pleaded guilty to intoxicated manslaughter and failure to stop and render aid. Montgomery County Judge Lisa Michalk sentenced Correa, giving him the maximum penalty on both counts, 20 years and 10 years, respectively.

21

Sgt. Brandon Mendoza

Age: 32
Location of Death: Tempe, Arizona
Killer: Raul Silva-Corona

On May 12, 2014, Officer Mendoza was headed home on U.S. 60, when he was hit head-on by an SUV driven by Raul Silva-Corona, 42, who was drunk and traveling in the wrong direction on the highway in Tempe, Arizona.

The website, America's Freedom Fighters, reported:

> It is unclear at this time whether or not Silva-Corona was ever deported, or was simply allowed to come and go across our currently unprotected border with Mexico.[1]

Mendoza was taken to a local hospital, where he died from his injuries. The illegal alien died at the scene of the crash.

Silva-Corona had a BAC of 0.238, nearly three times the legal limit, according to the Arizona Department of Public Safety.[2]

The 32-year-old officer was a thirteen-year veteran of the Mesa Police Department. He volunteered his time at the Boys and Girls Club, was an animal lover, and had recently fostered a homeless pit bull he named Lucy Blu.

It has been said that "a society can be judged by the way it treats its animals."

If that is true, Mendoza was as kind-hearted as he was brave.

On May 13, 2014, CBS 5 reported:

> Several months ago, he rescued a pit bull he'd found tied to a tree.
>
> Mendoza then saved her again when, after taking her to the county shelter, she was about to be put down due to kennel cough.
>
> "He took her in even though he wasn't sure she would be good with his little doxies," said Chandra Hardenburg who runs Pittie Me Rescue in Gilbert. "He had a heart for helping others, including our four-legged friends."
>
> Mendoza ended up fostering the dog he named Lucy Blu, through Hardenburg's organization, until she found a permanent home.
>
> "He was just a very caring person, human being and did a lot for his community, and it's just a sad day that he's lost his life," Hardenburg said.[3]

Brandon's mom, and his most-ardent advocate, Mary Ann Mendoza, was kind enough to sit down for an interview about her son, which follows:

Q: *Where were you and how did you find out your son had been killed?*

A: I was asleep. One of Brandon's fellow officers, who was also deployed to Afghanistan as he was in the Air National Guard, called me at around 3:00 am from his base. He told me Brandon had been in a bad accident. I got off the phone and tried calling Brandon over and over with no answer. At about 3:15, the doorbell rang and it was Mesa Police Department coming to get me and bring me to the hospital.

Q: *How has your life changed since this tragedy?*

A: Brandon and I were best friends. He is my third child out of four. He has two older brothers and a younger sister. A spoke of my family wheel is missing and will never roll smoothly ever again.

Brandon was not yet married and we traveled together, he invited me to a lot of events, dinners, and gatherings with his friends. I cannot tell you the heartache, loss, and tremendous grief I feel every day.

Every day consists of some sort of research, reaching out to others affected like me and calling on our politicians to wake up to the senseless, preventable tragedies happening in our country every hour of every day.

My vibrant, overachiever, loving, incredible son is gone!...I have nothing but memories of his beautiful face, his voice, his hugs, his laughter, his presence. In short, I am saddened by belief.

Q: *How was the issue that the killer was here illegally covered by the local media?*

A: It was not brought to life until a few days after Brandon was killed. The media is so sickening, and quite honestly, some police departments in our country cover this information up and make it almost impossible to gather the proper statistics that we need to report on the number of crimes committed daily, along with the number of Americans killed by illegal aliens.

Q: *What kind of person was Brandon? What were his goals, dreams, etc.?*

A: Brandon was a 32-year-old man at the time of his death, who had lived life to the fullest, never missed an opportunity to travel, be with family and friends, and made everyone feel like they were his best friend.

He was a modern beat cop who took time to meet each and every person in his beat by going door to door and creating relationships and cultivating trust. His beat prior to his death was an 8-10 city block area in south Mesa that he had been assigned to to clean up and get rid of drug dealers and homeless in the park. He took the assignment above and beyond what anyone expected of him. He was an overachiever. The stories I heard after his death, of things he had done for people, were mind-blowing! This young man was beyond the scope of what normal 32-year-olds are doing in this world, on top of having to discredit the stereotype thoughts most of a low-income area of town have of cops.

He loved to travel and was an avid photographer, and had an extremely large collection of black and white architectural photographs he took. He would take his photos, framed and matted, to First Fridays in downtown Phoenix and have a booth. He also made jewelry.

Brandon still met with one of his elementary school teachers several times a year and had lunch with her. He would go with low-income kids on his days off and play kickball and would buy them all pizza or ice cream after the game. He sponsored many children and families at Christmas with his own money. He rescued dogs and would help with placement with just the right person! His heart was huge and his personality left an impression on anyone who met him.

Q: *What would you like the public to know about this tragedy?*

A: I think you have all the details of how it happened. I would like the public to truly understand the depth of loss when a senseless tragedy occurs like this. This could have been avoided. This does not get to be our "new normal," and we cannot allow corrupt politicians or the illegal aliens thenselves to try and make us think this is okay in any way, shape, or form.

They are not here legally, we are not responsible for their well-being, and any politician who puts illegal aliens ahead of any American in any line or thought, needs to be removed from office.

There is absolutely no reason for any illegal alien criminal to be set loose and allowed to remain in our country after committing a crime. The leniency shown to illegal alien criminals in our country and justice system is sickening and broken. We need to secure our border and quit allowing these repeat criminals any way into our country.

22

Name: Ruben Morfin

Age: 13
Location of Death: Salinas, California
Killer: Ezequiel Mariscal

On December 29, 1990, Ruben was walking to his granddmother's house with a few friends, when a group of gang members began chasing them. The boys, including Ruben, began running in an attempt to flee to safety. Unfortunately, those gang members caught up with Ruben, and one of them, Ezequiel Mariscal, 20, shot him point blank in the back of his head.

Ruben was not a gang member, but just a young boy in the wrong place at the wrong time, in what was once a beautiful community that became infested with illegal alien gang members.

The wound was so devastating that a large portion of Ruben's brain actually exited his skull. He was taken to Salinas Valley Memorial Hospital, where he soon died.

Ruben was a seventh-grader at El Sausal Middle School.

Mariscal quickly escaped back to Mexico, where it took four long years, and the help of the television show "America's Most Wanted," to find him. However, due to Mexico's extradition policies, and the fact that the gang member could very well be facing the death penalty for his crime in this country, the governmnet of Mexico refused to return him to the United States, and instead he received a 20-year prison sentence in the state of Jalisco.

After losing her son, Angie Morfin became an activist, seeking to rid this country of illegal aliens.

On June 10, 1999, Angie testified before the U.S. House Subcommittee on Immigration. That testimony follows:

> Thank you Mr. Chairman and members of the committee. My name is Angie Morfin, I am a Latino-American woman from Salinas, California. I have come here today to tell you of a personal cost that I have paid for illegal immigration.
>
> But first I want to describe my community. Salinas is a community of 100,000 in Central California, it is not the big city. That part of California is a big agricultural area and so we have always had migrant farm workers. Years ago they would come and do the harvest and then leave once the work was completed. Now, they don't leave, and each year the number grows.
>
> We have a large community of illegal aliens, mostly Latino, and those numbers are growing, also. I can tell the members of this committee that the Latino-American citizens of our community want the illegals removed. We resent their presence in our community.
>
> At a congressional town hall meeting in Salinas last year, Congressman Sam Farr heard from many people from our community that they wanted more Border Patrol to catch and deport illegal aliens. Two sheriffs from neighboring counties told Congressman Farr that they wanted the Border Patrol to resume the practice of visiting their jails twice a week to remove and deport the illegals.
>
> Illegal immigrant crime is a real problem in my community. Gangs, illegal immigrant gangs, especially. We definitely have a need for increased enforcement. But even though we need it, and citizens have asked for it, the Salinas Border Patrol station has only one agent for a three county area. Just one. That is not the kind of commitment to immigration enforcement that is going to solve the problem in my community.

The price I have paid for nonenforcement of our immigration laws, and the presence of illegal aliens in my community was a big one. It is a price that I truly hope that none of you ever has to pay.

I told you that illegal alien gang activity is a problem in my community. Well in 1990 I found out how just how bad it could be when an illegal alien gang member from Mexico killed my thirteen-year-old son, Ruben. Ruben was not a gang member. He was just a beautiful little boy walking with some friends to his grandmother's house. As he and the others tried to run from the gang members who approached them, Ruben was shot in the head and killed. His killer fled the country, running back home to… Mexico. He was an illegal alien.

I was paralyzed with grief. I just wanted to die, I couldn't bear to live without my little boy. I cried and prayed to God for the strength to go on with my life. I prayed for justice for Ruben.

In the years that have passed since Ruben was killed I have met other mothers who have lost sons to gang violence, perpetrated by illegal aliens. I have sadly learned that this can happen to anybody. And while it is too late to protect my Ruben, it is not too late to take the measures necessary to make our communities safer and hopefully save someone else's child. Interior enforcement of our immigration laws will make our communities safer.

Ladies and gentlemen of the committee, it is not enough to talk about fixing the system. We must act, you must act now. And not just Congress, but all Americans need to get involved to solve the illegal immigration problem. I personally believe that more American Latinos should get involved. Together we can make a difference. The time has come for us as American-born Latinos, and all American citizens, to stand up for our rights as citizens.

Now I identified myself as a Latino-American woman at the beginning of this testimony. Actually, I don't like, or approve of hyphenated-Americans. We're Americans. And whether we are Latino-Americans, African-Americans, Asian-Americans, or European-Americans, the common denominator is that we are Americans. And it is our citizenship that we have in common. And as citizens we need

> to encourage you lawmakers to ensure that the laws you make are enforced, and that includes immigration laws.
>
> I thank God that I was born in this country and lived during a time when people are proud to be Americans. I am proud to say I'm an American. We should not be afraid to say how proud we are, or that we want to enforce our immigration laws and stop illegal immigration.
>
> Because, ladies and gentlemen, if we don't act like we care about this country we're not going to have a country.
>
> And, a nation that cannot control its borders won't be a nation for very long.
>
> I care about America and want to protect my country from illegal immigration.
>
> Thank you very much for inviting me to speak to you today.[1]

Angie has also shared her personal and painful experiences on Ruben's murder:

Q: *Where were you and how did you find out your son had been killed?*

A: I had just gotten home from work and I called my mother to see if Ruben was at her house. He was always at her house or mine. She was upset because my brother Mario had taken Ruben to a party and he didn't have a ride back. I asked her to please call me when he got home.

I had just laid down when my phone rang. I could hear my mother screaming "they shot the nino...they shoot the nino!" I knew in my heart that it was Ruben. She told me to get to the hospital. When I finally found him, they would not let me see my son. They wanted anyone but me to go in. I had other family members go into the room in order to identify him.

The doctor asked me if Ruben had any enemies, and told me it was as if they grabbed him by the shoulder and shoot him in the back of the head, point blank. The doctor said that he was dying and the only thing keeping him alive was the ventilator, that half of his brain had been blown out. They wanted to clean him up a little, so I could go in, but as I walked into the room, I could see my baby lying on the table. He had tubes all over him, and as I got closer, the doctor said "he is dying, we have to take him off of life support."

I said "please let me give him one last kiss, so he knows I'm here."

I gave him a kiss and they turned off the machine, I looked at my baby and I could see a tear drop fall from his eye and he died.

Q: *How has your life changed since this tragedy?*

A: Before Ruben was killed my life was simply family and my work was all that was important to me. I never really cared about anything else. After much work and saving, we bought our house and I just wanted my family to have a decent place to live. And our dreams were coming to pass.

After Ruben's death, my life changed forever. For years, I simply grieved. I could not come to terms with the fact that someone would hate my little boy so much that they could hurt him. My grief was unbearable; like my ancestors, I wore black clothes for more than ten years. Customs that were from an old age were brought back by those trying to help me. The candles, the Rosaries, the herbs that were burned during the ceremonies. I was heartbroken. The quietness of my life was shattered forever.

My child was shot by a stranger a block from my mother's house, in a spot that I must have passed a million times. It came to the point that I would go into panic attacks when I came near that place.

As I slowly came out of my fog, I became an activist against hate and violence. But, I found that those in charge wanted me to help with the gang violence erupting in our communities. I became a very strong voice. They wanted me, but also hated me because I just did not go their way. I stood my ground.

We had been raised to be good Democrats, but as I made the rounds I noticed more and more that it was only some Republicans who really cared and wanted to take action to stop the madness. The liberals who love to sing "Kumbaya," shake hands, and take pictures simply wanted to keep things the same.

Q: *How was the issue that the killer was here illegally covered by the local media?*

A: At first, I didn't know anything about the guy who murdered Ruben. All I was told was that he was from Huntington Park and not from Salinas, and he was here "visiting family members for the holidays." They said he didn't want to kill Ruben, but "only scare him."

One day, I started to notice that every time they talked about Ezequiel Mariscal they would say he was a "Mexican national," and that started to bother me. I learned that he was not in the country legally.

Q: *What kind of person was Ruben? What were his goals, dreams, etc.?*

A: Who was Ruben? Ruben was my life. He was my oldest child. He was my 'love-child.' His father was an American boy of Mexican parents. When I found out I was going to have a baby, my family encouraged me to find a good man and get married. I did marry and have more children. He loved them with all his heart.

Ruben had a heart of gold. He loved small children, and hated to see them cry. Ruben would do whatever it took to calm them down if they were crying.

He spent his time before and after school helping his grandparents with chores. When he wasn't doing that, he was playing baseball. Ruben loved the game. He would sign up every season and always excitedly told me about all of his games. He would invite me all the time, and drag my mom and dad with him to every game. My biggest regret was not finding the time to see him play more.

Q: *What would you like the public to know about this tragedy?*

A: My child is dead, for many years. For me, this life sentence is forever. I cry and grieve to this very day. When I finally woke up from the fog in which I was living, I found an old woman looking back at me and my babies were all grown up.

How was it possible that we are living in the greatest country in the world, and my child is shot and killed a block away from his grandmother's home? I thought for a long time that what happened to Ruben was my fault. But, as I walked through our justice system, I discovered that our elected officials had sold out our loved ones for their own gain.

I have met many important people...people who run this state and this nation. It makes me very sad that they don't care or think of us. I will keep the fight in my veins as long as I live, and I will try to protect my children and grandchildren from the DACA invasion.

For her activism and outspoken stance against illegal immigration, Angie has often been criticized and vilified by members of the Latino community.

On November 1, 2015, *Breitbart* reported:

> "I've been called a traitor," Morfin told the crowd gathered. She continued, "I think the best thing that's happened to us was Donald Trump."[2]

Angie was one of many then attending a National Remembrance Day rally for those killed by illegal aliens, held in Yorba Linda, California.

23

Officer Sheila Herring

Age: 39

Location of Death: Norfolk, Virginia

Killer: Mario Roberto Keen

On January 16, 2003, Officer Sheila Herring responded to a shooting at the Champion Sports Bar & Grill located at 1010 East Brambleton Avenue at 2:00 am.[1]

Mario Roberto Keen reportedly shot another man inside the bar.

Officer Herring arrived on the scene, along with other officers, and was shot three times by Keen. One of the rounds hit Herring in her abdomen, just below her protective vest. Other officers returned fire, killing Keen.

Herring was taken to Sentara Norfolk General Hospital, where she died in surgery, less than an hour later.

Keen, a Jamaican national, had been convicted in 1990 for the distribution of cocaine, made his way back into this country after being deported following completion of his sentence.

The Officer Down Memorial Page (ODMP) reported:

> Officer Herring was a U.S. Marine Corps veteran and had served with the Norfolk Police Department for 11 months. She had previously served three years with the Norfolk International Airport Police Department and 10 years with the Detroit, Michigan, Police Department.[2]

Officer Herring left behind an 18-year-old daughter.

On March 10, 2017, that young lady, now a grown woman with a child of her own, wrote on her mom's ODMP "reflections" section: "It's been forever since I've been on this site. I was thinking about you and decided to come here. I miss you so much. Your grandson constantly talks about you and he loves wearing a police T-shirt you had from Detroit. We love and miss you always and forever."

24

Emilee Olson, Hunter Javens, Jesse Javens, and Reed Stevens

Age(s): 9, 9, 13, and 12, respectively
Location of Death: Cottonwood, Minnesota
Killer: Alianiss Nunez Morales

In February 2008, four children were killed in Cottonwood, Minnesota, after their bus was hit by an illegal alien who ran a stop sign.

On a gloomy Tuesday morning, Guatemalan national, 23-year-old Olga Marina Franco Del Cid (a.k.a. Alianiss Nunez Morales) went sailing past a stop sign on County Road 24, and right into a school bus carrying 28 Lakeview School students. The bus flipped over on its side, injuring several children and killing four.

Hunter Javens Jesse Javens
Emilee Olson Reed Stevens

In addition to the children who were killed, four others were hospitalized at Avera McKennan Hospital and University Health Center in Sioux Falls, South Dakota. Another child was transported to the Mayo Clinic.

Apparently, the illegal alien was not even licensed to drive in her homeland of Guatemala. Lt. Mark Peterson of the Minnesota State Patrol told reporters: "She (Morales) doesn't have a driver's license anywhere that we're aware of."

On October 11, 2008, the website MASSCOPS.com, reported:

Olga Franco was charged with four counts of criminal vehicular homicide, running a stop sign, and driving without a license.

Franco, who drew nationwide attention from people focused on the illegal immigration debate, was found behind the steering wheel, her right foot wedged near the accelerator under a crumpled dash board.

She has maintained that her boyfriend was the one driving the van and that he fled because he didn't want to be deported to Mexico. Her attorneys argued at trial that he was thrown from the van on impact and Franco was thrown part-way into the driver's seat. The boyfriend is believed to be in Mexico.[1]

Of course, that was not the Guatemalan's first brush with the law. In 2006 she pleaded guilty in a Chippewa County court to driving without a license.

Franco, who originally gave police her alias, told investigators that she was on her way to work when she caused the fatal wreck. Despite her illegal status, she was employed by Norcraft Cabinetry in Eagan, Minn. The company's website (norcraftcompanies.com) displays a section entitled "Code of Business Ethics and Conduct."[2]

Within that section, the following statement is made: "All employees must respect and obey the laws of the cities, states, and countries in which we operate."

That statement seems more than a bit hypocritical coming from a company which hires illegal aliens!

In August 2008, a Kandiyohi County jury found Franco guilty on all counts, and she was subsequently sentenced to 12 and a half years in prison.

On April 26, 2016, Franco was sent to a halfway house (a non-Minnesota Department of Corrections facility) and released from custody on May 30, 2017. She was slated for deportation at that time, but ICE has yet to confirm if that action, in fact, took place.[3]

25

Rob Krentz

Age: 58
Location of Death: Cochise County, Arizona
Killer: Unknown

On March 27, 2010, Rob Krentz was shot to death near a watering hole on his 35,000-acre ranch. His mortally wounded dog, "Blue," also shot, was reportedly still trying to defend his master when the rancher's lifeless body was found.

Krentz's body was not discovered until shortly before midnight, which gave "the killer a nearly 14-hour head start to flee south to Mexico," reported The Arizona Capital Times. "He was likely long gone by the time they followed his tracks to the border the next afternoon."[1]

The motive for the murder was likely one of retaliation, as only a day before, his brother, Phil Krentz, phoned the Border Patrol to report drug smuggling activity on the ranch. As a result of the report, agents arrested eight illegal aliens and seized 290 pounds of marijuana.

The ranch, which has been in the Krentz family since 1907, is located in a known smuggling corridor.

Shortly after his body was discovered, U.S. Border Patrol agents, sheriff's deputies, and Department of Corrections dog chase teams followed a single set of foot tracks for 20 miles, to the Mexican border.

To this day, no one has been brought to justice for the Arizona rancher's murder, and despite reassurances from law enforcement, it appears that the case is very unlikely to ever be solved.

On October 31, 2013, the online magazine *Fronteras*, reported:

> Cochise County Sheriff Mark Dannels says the person of interest in connection with the murder of Robert Krentz is a resident of Cochise County....

> Dannels won't give many details about the person of interest. His name is Manuel Corona, and all that's known about him is that his 21-year-old son, also named Manuel Corona, has had violent encounters with law enforcement....
>
> In 2011, investigators identified a drug smuggler, Alejandro Chavez Vasquez, as another person of interest in the Krentz murder. That man, they believe, disappeared into Mexico.[2]
>
> The man who had worked his family's century-old ranch all of his life, and rather ironically, often provided assistance to those in need of food and water, even though they were illegal aliens, and even though they were trespassing on his property, has now been taken from his family and friends by one of those illegal aliens.

Rob's widow, Sue Krentz, has become an outspoken activist against illegal immigration, since her husband (below) was murdered.

In March 2016, Sue addressed "Calling Washington Home to the Border," a border enforcement rally in Animas, New Mexico, and spoke some very powerful words, as someone who has to re-live this ongoing tragedy every day.

The Arizona Daily Independent reprinted her speech:

> "If America was no different than any other country, we would not experience the relentless push to enter our

country from all parts of the world. We have been generous by providing aid to other countries, and by establishing a legal way to enter our country. Each of us expects to have a passport when we go to France," stated Krentz, referring to the fact that those who are crossing the southern border now have virtually no documentation.

"We expect our leaders to protect our nation and the citizens," continued Krentz. "All citizens support the government by paying taxes for protection and services. The phrase 'protect and serve' is painted on police cars. Safety and security is necessary to provide protection from potential threats, which are not limited to property, but also include animal welfare, crops, and health. All criminal activity threatens the safety of our society."

Quoting Ronald Reagan, Krentz said, "'We must reject the idea that every time a law is broken, society is guilty rather than the law breaker.' It is time to restore the American precept that each American is responsible for their actions."

Sue described the frustration of families living along

> the border. "We asked for help, and no one came. We requested a secure border and were told security was not to be expected. When we asked for safety, we were described as racist."
>
> "Border families have learned we cannot expect security. Our lives are at risk every day. We seem to be expendable and so too—our loved ones. When you have lost a family member to diseases or natural causes you have closure. When you lose that person by a violent act; to murder —it tears away a part of you. You remain injured and isolated. You cannot heal as the wound is raw with each report of the same criminal behavior. If you protest you face ridicule and are told to get over it. Which is impossible. You learn that you must live with this painful life lost through silent suffering."
>
> "The senseless murders of Kate Steinle, Brian Terry, and Rob Krentz made us realize that everything is different. The tragedy has changed our lives and the histories of our families forever. Secure the border for your family, and my family, and our community and our country. We are demanding the right to live free and safe—on our own land—and in our own homes."[3]

Adding to this widow's pain, in late September 2010, Sue was hit by a drunk-driving illegal alien, as she was leaving church services in Douglas, Arizona.

On October 2, 2010, *The White Mountain Independent* reported:

> The doctors have had to perform several operations to her pelvis and leg. She is currently in the ICU and stable. Her family is gathering in Tucson at the moment. They appreciate the outpour[ing] of concern from everyone. At this time, because of Sue's critical conditions, we ask that Sue receive no visitors and that we allow the family to be with Sue at this time. Please hold off on any cards and flowers at this time as Sue will not be able to receive them at the ICU.[4]

Fortunately, Sue is a very tough and determined lady and made a full recovery, and continues to fight for our immigration laws to be enforced.

26

Trooper Bret Clodfelter

Age: 34
Location of Death: Klamath Falls, Oregon
Killer: Francisco Manzo-Hernandez

On Sept. 30, 1992, Oregon State Trooper Bret Clodfelter stopped a suspected drunk driver who turned out to be an illegal alien named Francisco Manzo-Hernandez (a.k.a. "Poncho"). The drunk driver was traveling with two others. Trooper Clodfelter handcuffed the driver and placed him in the back seat of his cruiser.

After repeated calls from dispatchers to Clodfelter went unaswered, another trooper went to the scene and found him sitting in the front seat, dead. As all of the men were drunk, the state trooper offered to drive the two passengers home. For his kindness, Trooper Clodfelter was shot in the head four times.

Oregon.gov reported:

> [O]n the afternoon of October 2nd, 1992 an informant gave the location where Hernandez was hiding in a barn on the same street where he had shot & killed Trooper Clodfelter. The officers surrounded the barn & took him into custody as he climbed a fence and fled across a field.[1]

In February 1995, Manzo-Hernandez was convicted of murder and sentenced to life in prison.[2]

Trooper Clodfelter served with the Oregon State Police for eight years and left behind a wife, son, and daughter. A further tragedy took place a year after the trooper's murder, when his wife, Rene, took her own life.

27

Tony Bologna and his sons Michael and Matthew

Age(s): 48, 20, and 16, respectively
Location of Death: San Francisco, California
Killer: Edwin Ramos

On June 22, 2008, three members of the Bologna family were gunned down by Salvadoran native and MS-13 gang member, Edwin Ramos. The three men were shot dead in their car on a crowded street, in the city's Excelsior District.

Ramos, who is a member of the notoriously violent drug gang known as MS-13, shot the Bologna family to death because Tony Bologna had temporarily blocked the car in which Ramos was traveling, as the two cars made their way through an intersection. The Bologna men were returning home from a family barbecue.

Of course, San Francisco has a long-held "sanctuary policy" in place to shield illegal aliens from deportation; as such, city authorities failed to report Ramos to federal officials, despite his violent criminal history.

As a juvenile, Ramos brutally assaulted a man on a city bus, and within a few months of his release from a juvenile facility, committed a brutal robbery against a pregnant woman, which, then gave him two felony convictions.

Following his second conviction, he was sent to the Log Cabin Ranch, a camp run by the city for juvenile offenders, where he spent less than a year, and was released in February 2005.

While it is obvious that San Francisco's "sanctuary policy" played a major role in what ultimately led to the murders of Tony and two of his sons, there is apparently much blame to go around...

On July 20, 2008, *The San Francisco Chronicle* reported:

> [U]nder federal law, Ramos could have been referred to

> the Immigration and Customs Enforcement agency. But the Juvenile Probation Department's policy for dealing with offenders stipulated that "probation officers shall not discriminate in any fashion against minors based on their immigration status." If the department made any inquiries into whether Ramos was a legal U.S. resident, it did not pass along its findings to the federal government....
>
> Federal authorities finally learned that Ramos wasn't a legal U.S. resident sometime after he turned 18, when he applied for temporary residency status and was turned down. The records are confidential, so the exact date of Ramos' application is unclear, but Immigration and Customs Enforcement (ICE) spokeswoman Virginia Kice said that once he was turned down, he would have been considered deportable....
>
> When Ramos was arrested [for a third time], sheriff's deputies checked his immigration status on a national database and learned that he was considered deportable, immigration and sheriff's officials say. Eileen Hirst, chief of staff for Sheriff Michael Hennessey, said deputies had asked whether federal officials wanted to place a hold on Ramos so he could be taken into immigration custody.
>
> "In our communication with ICE, they specifically told us they were not placing a detainer on him," Hirst said. "We cannot hold people in custody without a documented reason to hold them."
>
> Kice acknowledged that federal authorities had not asked for Ramos to be held. She said she did not know why.[1]

At trial, the Bolognas' surviving son, Andrew, who was in the car and witnessed his father and two brothers killed, testified against Ramos.

CBS San Francisco reported on the dramatic courtroom scene:

"I saw him," Andrew Bologna said from the witness stand, pointing at Ramos. "He was staring at my dad, mugging him, giving him a mean look, and that's when he pulled out a gun."

Bologna, who was 18 at the time and is now 21, began crying as he recounted the shooting, which did not injure him.

"I didn't know what was going on, it was like a movie," he said. "They shot my family like that, it doesn't make sense."[2]

On June 10, 2012, Superior Court Judge Charles Haines sentenced Ramos for the three murders and one count of attempted murder, to three consecutive life terms in prison, without the possibility of parole. Because then-San Francisco District Attorney ruled out the death penalty in this case if Ramos was convicted, lie imprisonment was the maximum sentence the illegal alien could receive.[3]

Ramos and his attorneys have since appealed the conviction twice, and both times, his conviction was upheld.

Danielle Bologna filed a civil lawsuit against the city of San Francisco for protecting against deportation the illegal aliien gang member who ultimately took the life of her husband and sons.

However, in February 2010, San Francisco Superior Court Judge Charlotte Woolard dismissed the suit, claiming that the city's "sanctuary policy" was "intended to improve immigration controls, not to prevent crime," the San Francisco Gate reported.[4]

28

Dustin Inman

Age: 16
Location of Death: Ellijay, Georgia
Killer: Gonzalo Harrell-Gonzalez

On June 16, 2000, Dustin, along with his parents, Billy and Kathy, were on their way to a Father's Day weekend of camping and fishing, when their car was slammed into by a vehicle driven by Harrel-Gonzalez.

The Inmans were sitting at a stoplight when the crash occurred.

The television show "America's Most Wanted" with John Walsh, reported:

> Billy Inman's vehicle, a Pontiac Grand Am, was hit from behind. Billy Inman was stopped behind a Ford Bronco, which was stopped at a traffic light. Police say Gonzalo, who was driving an Oldsmobile, ran into Billy Inman's car. The speedometer of Harrell's vehicle was stuck at 62 mph. The impact from the rear-end collision pushed Inman's Pontiac into the rear of the Bronco, crushing it in an accordion-like fashion. Dustin Inman was sitting in the back seat along with his dog. Both he and his dog died at the scene. Police have stated that Gonzalo admitted to falling asleep in his car when he struck Inman's vehicle.[1]

Dustin was pronounced dead at the scene, while his parents both suffered serious injuries. In fact, Kathy spent the next five weeks in a coma, only to awaken to hear the news that her son was dead.

As a result of the spinal and brain injuries, Kathy Inman, has been confined to a wheelchair since 2000 and requires at-home nursing care, as well as frequent hospitalizations.

Because both were still hospitalized at the time, the two were unable to attend their son's funeral, and instead, had to watch the service for their only child on video.

As for the illegal alien who killed Dustin, he only suffered minor injuries in the wreck, and quickly left the North Georgia Medical Center and fled to his home country of Mexico.

Harrell-Gonzalez was charged in absentia with vehicular homicide, and remains a fugitive to this day.

On June 17, 2016, CBS 46 reported:

> The FBI considers Harrell an international fugitive from the law. The Department of Justice, however, recently confirmed there are legal loopholes that keep Harrell from being brought back to the U.S. to face charges.
>
> A portion of a recent DOJ letter sent to CBS 46 reads as follows:
>
> "The Department of Justice considers the extradition of fugitives one of our highest priorities and our attorneys in the Office of International Affairs (OIA) work closely with prosecutors in the United States and foreign authorities to locate and extradite fugitives. In this case, OIA attorneys have been in close contact with state prosecutors in Gilmer County about the matter. In December of 2015, OIA notified the Gilmer County prosecutor assigned to the case that vehicular manslaughter was not an extraditable offense under the U.S.-Mexico extradition treaty nor under Mexican law. The treaty requires, among other things, that the criminal conduct for which extradition is sought be classified as a crime in both countries and be specifically enumerated in the list of extraditable offenses contained in the treaty. Vehicular manslaughter is not an enumerated offense under the treaty and Mexican law does not criminalize vehicular manslaughter absent a showing of intent and/or malice to commit the crime, factors which do not appear to be present in this case. OIA also informed the prosecutor that extradition was not possible because the statute of limitations for prosecuting the offense under Mexican law had lapsed. Because these

> treaty requirements were not met, OIA determined that the extradition process could not proceed."
>
> "We know where the individual is in Mexico but we just can't get him back to the U.S.," Stephen Emmett, with the FBI, said. "This is a little bit of a strange territory that we find ourselves in. We're on the side of the family in wanting this individual returned."
>
> The FBI has said they are frustrated over the decision to not return Harrell to the U.S.[2]

The death of Dustin Inman spurred Atlanta-area businessman D.A. King to create the "Dustin Inman Society," and Mr. King continues to advocate not only for the Inman family, but for secure borders and the enforcement of this country's immigration laws.[3] Billy Inman has shared how this tragedy affected his life, and continues to do so in the following interview:

Q: *When did you realize that your son had been killed in the crash?*
A: About two weeks after the wreck, after our families had already buried Dustin, I was still in a daze, trying to find Kathy's family members, asking them questions, and talking to the doctors about Kathy. I was going back and forth to see Kathy every day, and I finally had to tell her about Dustin. But it really didn't sink in until September 13, the day I took Kathy to the cemetery for the first time. We had to watch the funeral on a VHS tape a family member made for us.

Q: *How have your lives changed since this tragedy?*
A: Of course, it has changed drastically. It's really not much fun anymore, just doctors appointments and physical therapy, trying to live daily. Kathy has got so much going on from her brain injury, I still take her to the doctors once or twice a week. She is slowing down more and more, and her pain level is steadily increasing. I don't know what to do really, I wish I could do something to help her, but the doctors keep saying there isn't much they can do about the scar tissue on her brain. And, nobody can do anything about our shattered dreams.

Q: *How was the issue that the killer was here illegally covered by the local media?*
A: At first, there was nothing in the Gilmer County paper where the wreck happened. Later, they did a story entitled "A Blue Christmas," about what happened to us. I got a letter to the editor in the paper, but no national news media coverage. I do want to thank D.A. King for starting the Dustin Inman Society, and for all he has done by helping me keep it alive.

Q: *What kind of kid was Dustin? What were his dreams, goals, etc.?*

A: He was a dang good kid! I was proud to be his daddy. He brightened up the room everywhere he went with a smile or his antics, trying to enjoy life even though he was born with a cleft lip and palate, he tried to smile everywhere he went. He loved life, family, friends, fishing, hunting, and eating.

He always told us he wanted ten kids one day, because he was an only child. I believe he would have. His orthodontist fell in love with him, and she offered to put him through medical school to help her in her practice; he seemed to really like the idea.

Q: *What would you like the public to know about this tragedy?*

A: It can happen to them too! Our dreams are shattered and there's so much in life we won't get to do. We're losing more than dollars, death is something we all have to face one day, but what happened to Dustin and my family is unacceptable. It's not right and something needs to be done. Gonzalo Harrell-Gonzalez is an illegal alien with no priors, using two social security numbers and one bogus resident alien card.

People need to open their eyes and look to see what's passing them on the road every day. Look at how much things have changed since we were kids. What will the future hold for everyone's kids and grandkids is what bothers me.

29

Mackenzie Maddox

Age: 6

Location of Death: West Allis, Wisconsin

Killer: Jose Rodriguez

On June 9, 2008, Mackenzie was hit and killed while crossing the street in a suburb of Milwaukee. The man behind the wheel was a previously deported Mexican national.

As the little girl and her mother crossed the street at S. 84th St. and W. Cleveland Ave. in West Allis, the dump truck driven by Rodriguez came speeding through the intersection, striking both the little girl and her mother Andrea. Mackenzie died at the scene and her mother was taken to Froedtert Hospital with serious injuries, but survived.

Rodriguez was charged in Milwaukee County Circuit Court with driving with a revoked license, causing death, a misdemeanor.

The illegal alien Rodriguez racked up multiple convictions in the Milwaukee area, including one for a DUI, according to police.

Only four months before killing Mackenzie, while serving a 30-day sentence in the Kenosha County Jail, Rodriguez was identified by ICE and deported back to Mexico.

Despite having no valid driver's license, multiple traffic convictions, and being in the country illegally, Rodriguez was working for an Oak Creek waterproofing business and was driving a company vehicle when he hit Mackenzie and her mom.[1]

A portion of Mackenzie's obituary follows:

> Mackenzie was very special to everyone. We miss you and love you. Mackenzie loved to play with her sister Emma and cousin Kamrin at grandpa and grandma's house. Mac loved to swim, ride her bike, play hide and seek and help mom bake and cook. She also enjoyed riding ponies and loved horses. She loved to play at McCarty Park and Riverside Park, and helped grandma plant flowers. Mac loved to camp with her family.[2]

Rodriguez was convicted and sentenced to nine months in prison, the maximum sentence possible.

30

Sarah Root

Age: 21
Location of Death: Omaha, Nebraska
Killer: Eswin Mejia

On January 31, 2016, Eswin Mejia slammed his pickup truck into the rear of Sarah Root's SUV that was stopped near the intersection of 33rd and L Streets. The 19-year-old Honduran national was reportedly street racing with another vehicle at the time of the crash.

Sarah died at the Nebraska Medical Center a few hours after she was extricated from her vehicle, having graduated only a day earlier from Bellevue University.

Mejia was taken to the same hospital with minor injuries, and a blood test revealed a Blood Alcohol Concentration (BAC) of .241, three times the legal limit.

He was charged with vehicular homicide and DUI. Despite the serious nature of the charges and the fact that he was in the country illegally, Mejia was freed on bond only a few days after killing Root.

The Daily Nonpareil reported:

> Mejia was freed Friday after paying 10 percent of the $50,000 bail amount set by Douglas County Judge Jeffrey Marcuzzo.
>
> The judge set bail on the condition that Mejia participate

> in a 24/7 sobriety program that requires him to appear twice a day for Breathalyzer testing.[1]

Of course, Mejia failed to show for the testing, and remains a fugitive at this time.

Douglas County is a "sanctuary" for illegal aliens, according to the Center for Immigration Studies.[2]

Mejia has a long history of arrests in Douglas County, and has often failed to appear in court. In fact, at the time Root was killed, the illegal alien had several warrants for his arrest, but was never reported to Immigration and Customs Enforcement (ICE), according to court records.

However, in the case of his latest arrest, Omaha Deputy Police Chief Dave Baker told RadioIowa that his department requested an ICE detainer, but one was never issued:

> As a local law enforcement agency, we're not empowered to enforce federal immigration laws; however, we do work with the immigration authorities on a federal level. In this case, the individual, Mr. Mejia, was in our country illegally. He was from Honduras. We do attempt to make sure the judge is aware the individual is in the country illegally, not on the basis of whether the individual is guilty or not guilty. It does not affect what charges they are charged with on a local or a state basis. It has to do with whether or not there is a flight risk. Our accident investigator did request a detainer; however, one was not issued or granted prior to him bonding out. His brother did bond him out before the detainer was issued. My understanding was that he was bonded out fairly quickly.[3]

Eswin Mejia entered this country in 2013 as an "undocumented minor," according to ICE.

A week after Sarah was killed, a candlelight vigil was held in her hometown of Council Bluffs, Iowa, at Bayliss Park.

Her father, Scott Root, addressed the crowd of about 100 mourners, saying: "We would like to draw attention, however, to the fact that we laid her to rest yesterday, and the cost of a bond cost less than a funeral."[4]

While ICE points the finger of blame at officials in Omaha, and, in turn local authorities claim otherwise, it is obvious that Sarah Root, along with her grieving family, was betrayed by more than one level of government.

31

Officer Rolando Tirado

Age: 37
Location of Death: Phoenix, Arizona
Killer: Cesar Tomas Quiroz-Leon

On May 1, 2011, Buckeye police Officer Rolando Tirado was killed and Officer Christopher Paz was left seriously wounded outside the El Gran Mercado in Phoenix. The officers were working a private security job at the time of the shooting.

The officers had just stopped a vehicle in the parking lot, and Officer Tirado was speaking to the driver outside of the vehicle, when the passenger sudenly jumped out and shot Officer Tirado from behind, according to Phoenix Police Sgt. Tommy Thompson.

That passenger was identified as Cesar Tomas Quiroz-Leon, 27. An online memorial operated by the Buckeye Police Department states:

> The gunman then engaged in a gunfight with the second officer, during which the gunman was shot and killed. The second officer, also from the Buckeye Police Department, was transported to a local hospital in critical condition with multiple gunshot wounds to his shoulder, neck, and lower body. Officer Tirado succumbed to his wounds and died at the scene.
>
> The driver of the vehicle was critically wounded during the gunfight, and a third occupant fled the scene but was captured two days later by the Phoenix Police Department.[1]

Officer Paz survived his wounds.

Prior to joining the Buckeye Police Department, Officer Tirado served with the U.S. Marine Corps, spent four years as a deputy with the Maricopa County Sheriff's Office, and as an officer with the Surprise Police Department.

During his seven years with the Buckeye Police Department, Tirado worked as a School Resource Officer and served as a crisis negotiator with the department's SWAT Team.

He left behind his wife Ana and two sons, Alec and Alden.[2]

32

Joshua Wilkerson

Age: 18
Location of Death: Pearland, Texas
Killer: Hermilo Moralez

On November 16, 2010, Joshua gave 19-year-old Hermilo Moralez a ride home, as he did on many days. The two attended the same high school.

When Joshua failed to return home, his parents contacted police. That evening, his mom, desperately searching for Joshua, found his abandoned pickup truck parked at a local strip mall.

The following day, Moralez confessed to killing Joshua and eventually agreed to lead them to the location of his body, a field in Fort Bend County. His hands and feet were bound and his body had been set ablaze.

A bloody stick which Moralez used to beat Joshua into unconsciousness was found near the illegal alien's home.

Click2Houston reported:

> Moralez was charged with murder, a first-degree felony, failure to identify, and attempting to take a weapon from a peace officer. Investigators said Moralez, while handcuffed, tried to pull a detective's weapon from his holster as they

> jumped a fence in a field. He was immediately restrained, police said. He also provided a false identity when he was questioned, officials said.[1]

On January 28, 2013, a Brazoria County jury found Moralez guilty of the brutal murder. He was sentenced to life in prison.[2]

Joshua's mom, Laura Wilkerson, has become a very outspoken advocate for the enforcement of immigration laws.

In July 2015, she testified before the U.S. Senate Judiciary Committee. A portion of that powerful testimony follows:

> My son's name was Joshua Wilkerson. On November 16, 2010, he was beaten, strangled, tortured until he died. He was tied up, thrown in a field, and set on fire. His killer, Hermilo Moralez, was brought here illegally by his illegal parents when he was ten years old, so he fit the "DREAM" kid description. He was sentenced to life in prison, which means it will be 30 years before he's up for parole. He'll be a 49-year-old man, who I don't expect to be deported. And I just hope he doesn't come to live in your city.
>
> We had to hear this kid on the stand muttering about, "In my country…" "In my country…" never to finish that sentence. We listened to him tell us repeatedly that his "killing skills took over," that Josh had kicked his dog, and his "killing skills took over." His parents somehow managed to provide lessons so he acquired a black belt in mixed martial arts. Joshua had never been in a fight in his life.
>
> Instead of getting Joshua home that day from school, we got an autopsy report.
>
> "This body is received in a grey body bag. There's a tag on his toe that bears the name, Joshua Wilkerson. This is a white male weighing a hundred pounds. He is tied up with braided rope — 13 loops around his neck in a slipknot. It goes behind his back through his back belt loop. It goes to his hands and his feet, behind his body. He has multiple fractures in his face and nasal cavity. His throat and his voice box are crushed."
>
> He was kicked so hard in the stomach that it sent his spleen into his spine, and sliced it in two… The medical examiner said it was torture.
>
> "This body has significant skin loss on his buttocks, his

> abdomen, his penis, his hands, and his face. He has one stick of gum and a tardy slip in his pocket."
>
> This was our family's 9/11 terrorist attack by a foreign invader, whether you want to recognize it or whether you do not," Wilkerson said. "This government continues to fail or even recognize that we have an issue. Americans are dying daily at the hands of criminals that we don't even know are here.
>
> You're officially notified today there's a problem when this happens. You can't deny it any longer. You cannot you cannot stand by and ignore our families — our American families. You're elected by Americans, not any other country. You should be for Americans.... If you want to sit quietly on the sidelines, you've thrown your hat into the ring already. Your silence speaks volumes. You're either for Americans, or you're not.
>
> I will not give up another one of my children so that a foreign person can have a nicer life. I'm not going to do it. You don't understand the pain. It's so deep in the soul — in the place you don't even recognize you have. There aren't words to describe the pain to someone who has not gone through it. I'm not giving up another kid.[3]

This writer completed the following interview with Laura Wilkerson about the torturous death of her beloved son:

Q: *Where were you and how did you find out your son had been killed?*

A: Joshua did not come home from school on November 16, 2010. It was so unlike him to not answer a call from me. I immediately knew something was very wrong. I began to look for him, went by his school and verified he was not there, then went by his friend Anthony's house. He told me he had not been able to get Josh on the phone either.

I continued looking and I found Josh's truck parked behind a strip center in town. It was parked next to a dumpster. The police came and marked it as a crime scene. They searched for Josh all night long until they found his body the next evening. The detectives came to our home and I said, "you found him" and they said "yes."

Q: *How has your life changed since this tragedy?*

A: My life has changed in every way you can imagine. At that instant, I became a different person. Every relationship I had ever had with anyone was changed. I lost my way. I became fearful, withdrawn, and impulsive. It felt like I was a newborn having to learn everything again, how to crawl, stand, think.

Q: *How was the issue that the killer was here illegally covered by the local media?*

A: In the beginning, the fact that Josh's killer was here illegally was not covered at all by the local news media. There were fake Facebook pages set up. Trolls from other countries saying horrible things about Josh, someone that they had never known. About 750 people came to say goodbye to Josh at the funeral. He was loved.

Q: *What kind of person was Joshua? What were his goals, dreams, etc.?*

A: Josh was a senior in high school, and he had talked with me about going into the United States Air Force. His older brother was serving at the time. Josh had a very soft heart for people. He was an old soul. He accepted Jesus Christ in his heart when he was 4 years old.

He had a relationship with Jesus, and had told me many times when he died he would be right with Jesus. He was an easy kid and had never been in trouble before. He was soft spoken and very respectful. He knew he would not live to be an older person. When Josh was younger I would tell him, one day that sky is going to open up and Jesus will be here to take us home. He always responded, "tell me again mama, tell me again."

Q: *What would you like the public to know about this tragedy?*

A: I want people to understand if this can happen in my "stay at home mom, take your kids to church, give them great values, blue collar, hard working family," it can happen to anyone. Evil is here and no one is exempt from it. The good news is we have a savior in Jesus. I could never have imagined murder being a part of my family. In Josh's case, had our border been secured and our immigration laws upheld, Josh may very well be here today. This has forever changed the lives of so many. We will never be the same again.

33

Deputy David March

Age: 33
Location of Death: Irwindale, California
Killer: Armondo Garcia

On April 29, 2002, Los Angeles County Deputy David March made a routine traffic stop near the intersection of Live Oak and Peck Road, around 10:39 a.m., and was shot to death.

The Los Angeles Sheriff's Professional Association reported:

> The driver of the vehicle exited his car and met the deputy halfway between the patrol car and the suspect's vehicle. A confrontation ensued between the deputy and the suspect. The suspect produced a handgun and fired at the deputy several times, striking him in the upper torso. The suspect fled the scene eastbound on Live Oak Avenue to southbound San Gabriel River (605) Freeway, and out of sight.[1]

Garcia reportedly told friends that he wanted to kill a police officer, and when he saw Deputy March on patrol that fateful evening, he intentionally pulled over and waited for March.

After the illegal alien murdered March, he quickly fled back to Mexico.

For four years, the government of Mexico refused to apprehend or extradite Garcia. In February 2006, U.S. Marshals arrested Garcia in Mexico. Garcia pleaded guilty and was sentenced to life in prison.

March served with the Los Angeles County Sheriff's Department for seven years. He left behind a wife and stepdaughter.

A memorial plaque was erected on Live Oak Avenue, in honor of Deputy March, which reads: "In memory of David W. March…Who made the ultimate sacrifice while protecting the citizens of Los Angeles County…A Hero never to be forgotten."

Every year on the anniversary of Deputy March's death, deputies take turns working 30-minute shifts in a 24-hour vigil in front of Temple Station, where March was assigned.[2]

34

Christopher "Buddy" Rowe

Age: 4
Location of Death: Santa Rosa, California
Killer: Marcos Lopez Garcia

On August 18, 2011, Christopher Rowe, along with his two sisters and mom, was walking to soccer practice, when he was struck in a crosswalk by a Honda Accord, driven by Mexican national, Marcos Lopez Garcia.

The impact was so great that it hurled Christopher's tiny body 80 feet, according to investigators.

The illegal alien quickly fled the scene and jumped into another car driven by his girlfriend. He was apprehended with the help of a citizen, Leroy Flach, who followed Garcia and phoned the information into police.

The following day, the little boy died from his injuries at Children's Hospital Oakland.

Garcia was charged with felony hit-and-run, vehicular manslaughter and driving without a license and booked into the Sonoma County Jail on an immigration hold.

The illegal alien pleaded guilty to all of the charges.

Garcia had two previous arrests for driving without a license, with the most recent arrest coming only five days before he hit Christopher, according to Santa Rosa Police Sgt. Rich Celli.[1]

On June 29, 2012, Sonoma County Superior Court Judge Kenneth Gnoss sentenced Garcia to four years in prison. He was deported upon his release.

A month after her son was killed, Michelle Rowe told *The Press Democrat*:

> Jim and I still sob at night, but the fact is we have two beautiful girls ... we got to keep going. We have this hole and deadness, but we know we have to participate.[2]

Christopher's obituary contained the following emotional tribute to the 4-year-old:

> Christopher was a special gift from God. From the moment he came to life, everyone knew he was something special. He will be remembered as an energetic, curious, active young boy with an ever-present smile, beautiful steel blue eyes and peaceful loving nature. He had just begun to show himself as a playful and imaginative storyteller who delighted both children and adults. He was always kind, compassionate, and caring, especially with his twin sister.[3]

35

Officer Nick Erfle

Age: 33
Location of Death: Phoenix, Arizona
Killer: Erik Jovani Martinez

On September 18, 2007, Officer Erfle and his partner stopped a group of men who were obstructing traffic. One of the men, Mexican national Erik Martinez, gave the officers a fictitious name in an attempt to hide his outstanding warrants.

When they attempted to take the illegal alien into custody, Martinez turned and shot Officer Erfle twice in the back of the head.

Officer Erfle was transported to Banner Good Samaritan Medical Center, where he was pronounced dead an hour later.

Martinez then fled the scene and committed a carjacking, in which the driver was held hostage.[1]

Shortly thereafter, officers caught up with Martinez, and he was shot to death. The hostage was unharmed.

At the time he shot Officer Erfle, Martinez had already accumulated a lengthy criminal history, which included a felony warrant for his arrest for aggravated assault. Martinez was deported in March of 2006 on theft charges, but obviously had no trouble re-entering the country illegally.

Officer Nick Erfle, was an eight-year veteran of the Phoenix Police Department, and left behind a wife and two children, according to his obituary.[2]

Ironically, Officer Erfle fought his way succesfully through two bouts of cancer, to return to the work he loved so much, protecting and serving the citizens of his hometown, only to be gunned down by someone who had no right to even be in this country.[3]

36

Officer Andrew Widman

Age: 30
Location of Death: Fort Myers, Florida
Killer: Abel Arango

On July 18, 2008, Fort Myers Police Officer Andrew Widman responded to a domestic disturbance call outside a local convenience store. That's when he encountered Cuban national Abel Arango arguing with his girlfriend in a nearby alley.

Arango immediately turned his anger upon Officer Widman, pulling a 9mm pistol from his pants and shot the officer in the face.

Officer Widman quickly succumbed to the point-blank shot, and Arango fled the scene as other officers began racing to the scene.

Several officers gave chase and a running gun battle ensued. The bloody episode was finally ended when an officer's .40 caliber round fatally found Arango in the neck at the intersection of Broadway and Main Street.

At a press conference shortly after Officer Widman was killed, Fort Myers Police Major Doug Baker said witnesses reported hearing Arango say "he was going to go out Miami-style, and he was going to take one of our officers with him."

Arango had a long history of arrests, including one only two months before he murdered Officer Widman, for selling cocaine. However, despite the fact that he was a foreign national and in violation of his probation, he was allowed to go free on bail.[1]

The Naples Daily News reported:

> From 1999 to 2004, he served time in prison for a holdup. After his release, on March 1, 2004, he began serving 15 years of supervised probation. But records show he stopped reporting to his probation officer and became a fugitive.
>
> An arrest warrant for violation of probation was issued in May, after Arango was arrested and charged in Lee County with two counts each of possessing cocaine and selling cocaine and one count of trafficking cocaine....
>
> As to why, in spite of a lengthy criminal record, Arango wasn't deported, U.S. Immigration and Custom Enforcement officials said it was out of their hands.
>
> In a statement released Monday, U.S. Immigration and Custom Enforcement (ICE) officials said Arango was released on an order of supervision in 2004 based on a 2001 Supreme Court ruling.[2]

As in so many cases, the federal government as well as local governments keep themselves busy blaming one another for another criminal alien who 'slipped through the cracks' of bureaucracy, while yet another innocent American is laid to rest.

Prior to joining the Fort Myers Police Department, Officer Widman served overseas as a Christian missionary. He served the citizens of Fort Myers for one year and three months, until his death.

On July 20, 2008, Officer Widman's family issued the following statement:

> The Widman family and the Rickards family would like to express our sincere gratitude and appreciation for the tremendous outpouring of support we've experienced over the last few days. Words cannot express how grateful we are for the cards, letters, meals, and errands run for the family while we prepare for the funeral. It's truly amazing the level of support we're experiencing. A special thank you to the men and women of the Fort Myers Police Department, the Lee County Sheriff's Office, and the Cape Coral Police Department for the unending dedication to the cause of taking care of Susanna and the three children Andy left behind. Thank you.

> Andrew Widman was a good man, a man who spent his life in service to others. Ultimately, he gave his life in that service. His friends, family, and coworkers will sorely miss him.
>
> Andrew was a strong Christian devoting much of his life to the pursuit of a calling in the ministry. He went to college to earn a Bachelor's Degree in Biblical Languages, followed by a Master's of Divinity Degree at Gordon Conwell Theological Seminary in Boston. After that, Andrew and Susanna desired to serve as missionaries in Thailand. However, after three years of support-raising efforts and moves from Massachusetts to Ohio and Florida, they prayerfully decided that Andrew would pursue a career as a police officer. Andrew was hired by the Fort Myers Police Department and completed the academy in September of 2007.
>
> Being a policeman was more than just a way to provide an honorable living for his wife and children. Police work was a continuation of the life of service Andrew had already led up to that point. By serving others Andrew was serving God in the process. His mission field turned out to be the streets of Fort Myers. He truly loved his job and planned to remain in the force as a career officer.
>
> Andrew leaves behind three children, ages 4 years, 20 months and 5 months. His wife Susanna Widman, daughter of Tommy and Bonnie Rickards of North Fort Myers survives him, as well as his parents Joseph and Martha Widman of Toledo, Ohio, his sisters Abby and Alyse, and his brother Tony.[3]

Fort Myers Mayor Jim Humphrey said it was "one of the saddest days in the life of this city," reported *The Naples Daily News*.

37

Detective Donald Young

Age: 43
Location of Death: Denver, Colorado
Killer: Raul Gomez-Garcia

On May 8, 2005, Detective Young and Officer John Bishop were working as uniformed security at a baptism reception at the Salon Ocampo Hall on West Mississippi Street. As the party was ending and guests were beginning to exit, previously deported Mexican national Gomez-Garcia opened fire on the two officers.

Officer Bishop was shot in the back, treated for his wounds at Denver Health Medical Center, and was later released.

Detective Young was shot three times, including once in the head. He was pronounced dead approximately one-half hour later at Denver Health Medical Center.

The Denver Post reported:

> Lt. Tony Lopez, who often worked with Young at Salon Ocampo, said Young worked Saturday at the downtown Cinco de Mayo celebration before heading to his off-duty job.
>
> Lopez said officers rarely had problems at Salon Ocampo and that the parties are usually joyous occasions.
>
> "It's normally a very happy time," Lopez said. "This guy came in with the intent to murder."
>
> "I don't think Donnie ever knew what happened. I don't think he ever saw it coming," Lopez said. "He was

> murdered. I don't know why someone would do something this cowardly and dastardly to a man as fine as Donnie."[1]

After ambushing the two officers from behind, Gomez-Garcia fled the scene and quickly made his way back to Mexico. He was taken into custody on June 5th, 2005, on the western coast of Mexico, by U.S. Marshals and Mexican federal police.

Gomez-Garcia was brought back to Denver, where he was convicted of second-degree murder and attempted second-degree murder. On October 25, 2005, he was sentenced to 48 years for Det. Donald Young's death and 32 years in prison for the shooting of Officer Bishop, for a total of 80 years to run consecutively.

In a demonstration of the illegal alien's callous attitude and complete disregard for human life, Gomez-Garcia was ushered into the courtroom shortly before his sentencing and asked if wanted to attend the proceeding. The Mexican national declined, but had shaved the number "13" into his hair, in one last attempt to spit in the face of Young's widow, his children, and fellow officers.

"His lawyers were trying to stay in front of him so we couldn't see clearly what he had in the back of his head," [Denver's District Attorney Mitch] Morrissey said. "But I could see the 13, and it is an affiliation with an L.A. gang that he had. It was not something that came up during the course of the trial, but obviously it is something he is very proud of today."[2]

Det. Donald "Donnie" Young served 12 years with the Denver Police Department, and left behind his loving wife Kelly and his two daughters Kourtney and Kelsey.

Of course, while then-Denver Mayor John Hickenlooper expressed his "outrage" at Young's murder, it should be noted that Hickenlooper also wholeheartedly embraced that city's "sanctuary policy" toward illegal aliens.

38

Officer Marc Atkinson

Age: 28
Location of Death: Phoenix, Arizona
Killer: Felipe Petrona-Cabana

On March 26, 1999, Officer Atkinson was following a Lincoln Continental, inside which sat a group of Mexican drug smugglers. As the Lincoln turned the corner, the driver, Felipe Petrona-Cabana, 17, jumped out of the vehicle and ambushed Officer Atkinson, firing several .357 rounds at his marked cruiser.

Officer Atkinson was struck twice in the head and crashed his patrol car into a telephone pole. He was soon pronounced dead at St. Joseph's Hospital and Medical Center.

APBnews.com reported:

> Rory Vertigan, 27, a night security guard who was driving by, witnessed the incident and fired on the gunman with his own semiautomatic weapon, hitting Petrona-Cabana in the left shoulder, [Detective Mike] McCullough said.
>
> As the man collapsed, two passengers, Oscar Garcia-Martinez and Oberlin Cabanas-Salgado, rushed out of the back seat and attempted to hide, but police caught one in a business across the street and the other a few blocks away, police said.[1]

A pound of cocaine was discovered in the suspects' vehicle.

All three were in the country illegally and were booked into the Maricopa County Jail on Immigration and Customs Enforcement (ICE) holds.

Petrona-Cabana was charged with first-degree murder, attempted murder, and aggravated assault. Garcia-Martinez and Cabanas-Salgado were charged with illegal possession of a firearm.

At the time of Officer Atkinson's murder, Garcia-Martinez had outstanding warrants on several drug charges.

Officer Atkinson served with the Phoenix Police Department for five years, and left behind a wife and his infant son.[2]

39

Officer Vincent Owen D'Anna

Age: 26
Location of Death: Flint, Michigan
Killer: Ramon Felix Pineda

On August 26, 2007, drunk-driving Mexican national Ramon Felix Pineda hit Flint Police Officer D'Anna, who was riding his motorcycle off-duty. Pineda actually dragged Officer D'Anna, who was pinned under his IROC Camaro, for some distance along Sashabaw Road in Independence Township.

Pineda jumped from his car and fled on foot, until he was apprehended by a citizen.

The next day, officer Vincent Owen D'Anna succumbed to his injuries at Genesys Hospital.

Pineda, who had been living in the country illegally for ten years under several aliases, at the time of the deadly crash had a Blood Alcohol Concentration (BAC) of .16, twice the legal limit.

Witness Larry Hartley watched the Camaro hit D'Anna's motorcycle multiple times.

"As it hit the bike's tire, the Camaro was pulling on the back end of the bike," he said. "It was like a monster swallowing something up, taking a bite, taking a bigger bite, and pretty soon the car was on top and the guy on the bike was completely under the car," reported *The Clarkston News*.[1]

Pineda was charged with second-degree murder, driving while intoxicated causing death, failure to stop at the scene of an accident, operating a vehicle with a suspended license, and false certification of personal information to obtain a driver's license.

Officer.com reported:

> D'Anna was wearing a helmet at the time of the crash. The 26-year-old Goodrich resident had graduated from Clarkston High School in 1999 before receiving his bachelor's degree in criminal justice from Ferris State University in 2005. His first position with a law enforcement agency was with the Flint Police Department, which hired him in 2005.[2]

During his arraignment, Oakland County Sheriff's Lt. James Ahearn told the court that Pineda admitted to drinking seven beers before getting behind the wheel, and was simply driving too fast to slow down.

As if to rub salt in the wounds of Officer D'Anna's grieving family, Pineda's defense attorney, Arthur Greenstone, asked the court for bond for his client, and cited "a language barrier," as a mitigating factor.

"His 1-year-old son and his wife are here. It appears this is a one-time incident, and it is awful, but there is no history of substance abuse or violence," Greenstone told the court. "If you scratch this catastrophe, you will find someone who has been a productive member of this community," *The Oakland Press* reported.[3]

On June 4, 2008, Oakland County Circuit Judge Wendy Potts sentenced Pineda to 28 to 70 years in prison for second-degree murder, and also ordered Pineda to spend an additional 10-15 years in prison for drunken driving causing death, and up to another five years behind bars for failing to stop at an injury accident.

Commenting on the sentence, Keith Speer, president of the Flint Police Officers Association, stated: "No amount of years is going to bring Vince back but it sounds like a pretty just sentence," reported Mlive.com.[4]

40

Scott Gardner

Age: 33
Location of Death: Brunswick County, North Carolina
Killer: Ramiro Gallegos

On July 16, 2005, Scott and Tina Gardner were headed to the beach for a long-awaited vacation with their two young sons, Avery and Jackson, when habitual DUI offender Ramiro Gallegos crossed the center line and slammed head-on into the Gardners' vehicle.

Both Scott and Tina were taken to New Hanover Regional Medical Center in Wilmington, where Scott underwent surgery and died a few hours later. Tina suffered major head trauma, and as a result now resides in a nursing home, suffering from traumatic brain injuries.

Their two children, 5-year-old Jackson and 2-year-old Avery, suffered only minor injuries and have been raised by their grandparents.

Gallegos was charged with second-degree murder, assault with a deadly weapon, habitual impaired driving, felony hit-and-run, driving with a revoked license, driving while under the influence, reckless driving, and failure to wear a seat belt.

On February 17, 2006, Gallegos was allowed to plead guilty to second-degree murder in exchange for a lesser sentence.

Brunswick Superior Court Judge William C. Gore, Jr. sentenced the illegal alien to 14 years to 18 years in prison.

Despite the fact that he was in the country illegally, Gallegos had been convicted of three DUIs in North Carolina, and twice more outside of the state, before he killed Gardner.

He was deported once back to Mexico, but was back in the country within six months.

Incredibly, Gallegos was charged with a DUI in 2002, but when he failed to show for his court appearance, the charges were dismissed. He was later convicted that same year on a separate DUI in Duplin County, and sentenced to probation.

WRAL reported:

> He has three previous [DUI] convictions, but none resulted in his deportation. His stiffest sentence was handed down by a Brunswick County judge in 2004. That judge sentenced Gallegos to a maximum sentence of two years, but suspended that sentence and allowed Gallegos to serve only 30 days in jail over 15 weekends. He also ordered 30 months probation.[1]

In response to Gardner's murder, and the complete disregard for the public's safety demonstrated by our local, state, and federal governments in regards to dangerous illegal aliens, former Rep. Sue Myrick (R-NC) introduced the Scott Gardner Act.[2]

On March 7, 2012, Rep. Myrick re-introduced the measure before the Committee on the Judiciary Subcommittee on Immigration Policy and Enforcement. What follows is a portion of her statement to the committee:

> Chairman Gallegly, Ranking Member Lofgren, and Members of the Subcommittee, thank you for inviting me and my colleague Representative Mike McIntyre here today. And thank you for holding a hearing on what we feel is a vital piece of legislation—the Scott Gardner Act.
>
> On July 16, 2005, Scott Gardner, his wife Tina, and their two children were on their way to Sunset Beach. Scott was a high school Social Studies teacher from Gaston County, and as is customary during the summer break from school, many Carolinians make a trip to the coast.
>
> However, while the Gardner Family was in Brunswick County, their car was struck by Ramiro Gallegos, an illegal immigrant who was driving drunk. Scott Gardner was killed. Seven years later, Tina Gardner remains in a vegetative state.

> After the accident, it was discovered that Gallegos had been previously arrested five times—*five times*—for drunk driving. The accident on July 16, 2005, was not his first alcohol-related accident. In 2002, he was involved in a head-on collision. Two of the previous arrests were outside the state of North Carolina.
>
> Once, he was deported back to Mexico. However, six months later, he was back in the United States with a Michigan driver's license. After his other arrests, he was either released on probation, or served minimal time in jail—up to thirty days—before being released and asked to show up in court. He never did.[3]
>
> Sadly, this is not an isolated incident....
>
> Since 2005, I have reintroduced the Scott Gardner Act every Congress.
>
> Very simply, HR 3808 does three things:
>
> First, it amends the Immigration and Nationality Act to allow local or state law enforcement officers to issue a federal detainer for any individual who is in the country illegally and has been arrested for driving while intoxicated. Officers would be allowed to confirm immigration status via national databases if reasonable evidence exists that the arrested individual is in the country illegally.
>
> Second, the bill requires that the Department of Homeland Security reimburse local law enforcement for the cost of transferring any such individual(s) into federal custody.
>
> Lastly, the bill requires that DHS prioritize the deportation of any illegal immigrant arrested for DWI.[3]

Every year, between 2005 and 2012, Rep. Myrick introduced the Scott Gardner Act in an effort to make our streets safer. And, every one of those years, our Congress failed to pass it.

In January 2013, the popular Republican Congresswoman retired.

Scott's mom, Emily Moose, sat down for the following interview about her son's death:

Q: *Where were you and how did you find out your son had been killed?*

A: On July 15, 2005, I spent the day with my son and his wonderful wife and amazing children. His son, Jackson, was 5 years old and his daughter, Avery, was 2 years old. They were going to their first vacation the next day since their daughter was born, so I spent the day with them, having fun and buying beach toys for my grandkids. The reason Scott and Tina had not had a vacation for two years was because Avery was born 27 weeks premature, and their caring for her and their financial burden was very heavy. On July 16, 2005, as my precious children were heading to Surf Side Beach they were crashed into, head-on, by a drunk illegal. My son died nine hours later, and my wonderful daughter-in-law, Tina, is still, 13 years later, in a permanent vegetative state. My grandchildren suffered minor injuries, but have lost their parents due to the lack of law enforcement.

The day the horrible crime happened, I was at work in Rock Hill, South Carolina. When I got home around 6 p.m., I got a phone call and was told that I needed to come to Wilmington as soon as possible. I was informed that Scott and Tina were airlifted to Wilmington and things did not look very good. None of our family were close by, and it took me five hours to get there. My grandchildren were at another hospital and could not be released until someone in the family arrived. My sister and her daughter left from Greensboro to get my grandchildren, while I was at New Hanover Hospital waiting for my son to get out of surgery. Scott died at 3 am.

Q: *How has your life changed since this tragedy?*

A: My life has never been the same. Not only have the grandparents had to support, care for, and raise our two babies, we have had to care for Tina. She has been in a nursing home for 13 years. The criminal that did this to our family, has never been charged with the crimes that left Tina in the horrible state that she is in.

Q: *How was the issue that the killer was here illegally covered by the local media?*

A: The local news media did some coverage of the tragedy, I was interviewed many times by North Carolina news stations and by Fox News. I went to Washington several times to testify at Congressional hearings, and pleaded for support of The Scott Gardner Act. The Act was passed by the House of Representatives, but the Senate never even considered it. The WRAL documentary *Crossing the Line* was put out by Focal Point December 5, 2007.

Q: *What kind of person was Scott? What were his goals, dreams, etc.?*

A: Scott was an amazing man. He was a devout Christian, he loved his family so much and loved his profession. He was a teacher and head baseball coach. He told me that his career gave him the chance to share God's word with youngsters. Scott has many memorials, the site where the tragedy happened, his college, Charleston Southern University, the high school where he taught and coached.

Our whole family's life has changed, life as we expected was taken away. The man that did this to us was in front of a judge 5 times for DUI. He was deported 3 times but he never was punished for the crimes he committed until he stole an innocent life.

Q: *What would you like the public to know about this tragedy?*

A: All Americans should know that these criminals get far more support and government assistance than we, the victims do. After Scott passed away, even with the life and health insurance he had, we were billed $89,000 by the hospital. The illegal alien was caught and treated at the same hospital, and was never sent a bill.

SCOTT GARDNER ACT

HEARING
BEFORE THE
SUBCOMMITTEE ON
IMMIGRATION POLICY AND ENFORCEMENT
OF THE
COMMITTEE ON THE JUDICIARY
HOUSE OF REPRESENTATIVES
ONE HUNDRED TWELFTH CONGRESS
SECOND SESSION
ON
H.R. 3808

MARCH 7, 2012

Serial No. 112–96

Printed for the use of the Committee on the Judiciary

Available via the World Wide Web: http://judiciary.house.gov

U.S. GOVERNMENT PRINTING OFFICE
WASHINGTON

Our family has had to pay very high insurance bills and medical bills for Tina, Jackson, and Avery. The illegals get free medical coverage, and we were informed that the family of the man who killed my son was on food stamps and housing assistance. Victims are never assisted in any way by our own government. I have been threatened, called a racist, and verbally assaulted by many since becoming an advocate to help save and protect others from this preventable type of tragedy.

41

Jamiel Shaw

Age: 17
Location of Death: Los Angeles, California
Killer: Pedro Espinoza

On March 2, 2008, as 17-year-old Jamiel Shaw was walking home from the Beverly Center Mall, Pedro Espinoza, an illegal alien gang member, pulled alongside the teenager and asked him what gang he was in. According to witnesses, the high school football standout did not answer him. He did not answer because he had no part of gang life.

Espinoza then opened fire on Jamiel, hitting him once in the abdomen, and while he lay on the ground bleeding, the illegal alien shot him once again, in the face. Jamiel was only three blocks from his home.[1]

His father, Jamiel Shaw, Sr., actually heard the gunshots and ran outside to find his son lying, bleeding to death on the ground.

Jamiel was taken to a local hospital, where he was pronounced dead a short time later.

At the time of his murder, Jamiel's mom, Anita Shaw, was serving her second deployment in Iraq with the U.S. Army. She returned home for his funeral.

Pedro Espinoza was a member of L.A.'s notorious 18th Street Gang, and had a history of arrests for weapons charges and even a conviction for assault on a police officer. Despite his violent criminal history and the fact that he was in the country illegally, he was never reported to federal immigration authorities.

Of course, in 1979, Los Angeles officials initiated "Special Order 40," which prevents the police from inquiring into suspects' immigration status, thus making Los Angeles a "sanctuary city," and protecting illegal aliens from possible deportation.[2]

On May 9, 2012, Espinoza was found guilty of first-degree murder. Several months later, Los Angeles County Superior Court Judge Ronald Rose sentenced the illegal alien to death. He currently sits on California's crowded death row.

On the day of his sentencing, *The Los Angeles Times* reported:

> Pedro Espinoza took pride in his gang affiliation.
>
> The 18th Street gang member, with slick black hair and tattoos on his neck and arms, once bragged to a parole supervisor that he aspired to land on death row for his allegiance, prosecutors said.[3]
>
> In 2009, the Shaw family filed a wrongful death suit against Los Angeles, also naming Los Angeles County Sheriff Lee Baca as a defendant in the suit. In 2010, Los Angeles Superior Court Judge Charles F. Palmer threw out the suit, claiming government officials had "legal immunity" in such cases.
>
> In 2008, in response to Jamiel's murder, attorney and former L.A. mayoral candidate, Walter Moore, drafted what is known as "Jamiel's Law." The proposal would "deny

ABOUT JAMIEL

Jamiel Andre' Shaw, II "Jas" Was a Happy Teenager!

Jas is loved by so many!! He had a smile that could light up your heart. He was only 17 years young when his life was suddenly taken.

Jas was brutally assassinated on March 2, 2008. In the early evening of March 2nd, Jas was returning home from the Beverly Center Mall. He was walking from the bus stop when his father (Jamiel Sr.), called him on his phone, "Be right home dad, I'm right around the corner old man", he said. He was just three houses from his home when he was assassinated.

sanctuary city protection to any illegal aliens in gangs in the city of Los Angeles."[4]

Moore, along with the Shaw family, attempted to gain enough support for it to become a ballot initiative, but the measure failed.

The Shaw family continues the fight to pass "Jamiel's Law."

Because of Jamiel's ability on the football field, he was being scouted by both Rutgers and Stanford Universities. He also played baseball and basketball, as well as the piano, and by all accounts had an outstanding future ahead of him.

Of course, all of that potential came to a screeching halt on March 2, 2008.

42

Officer Shane Figueroa

Age: 25
Location of Death: Phoenix, Arizona
Killer: Salvador Vivas-Diaz

On October 25, 2008, Officer Figueroa was responding to a "shots fired" call when his patrol car was hit by a pick-up truck driven by Mexican national Salvador Vivas-Diaz. The impact of the crash sent the officer's patrol car spinning into a cinder block wall.

Officer Figueroa was thrown from the vehicle upon impact. He was transported to St. Joseph's Hospital and Medical Center, where he was soon pronounced dead.

Vivas-Diaz had a history of DUI arrests and had been previously deported. He was drunk at the time he hit Officer Figueroa.

At the time of the crash, the illegal alien had four outstanding warrants against him.[1]

Vivas-Diaz was charged with manslaughter and aggravated assault.

On June 26, 2009, the Maricopa County Attorney's Office issued the following press release:

> County Attorney Andrew Thomas announced today that Salvador Vivas-Diaz (DOB 9/17/58) has been sentenced to 16 years in prison for causing a crash that claimed the life of Phoenix Police Officer Shane Figueroa.

> On October 25, 2008 Officer Figueroa was responding to an emergency call when Vivas-Diaz made a left turn in front of the officer near 19th Ave and Roeser. The officer was ejected from his police cruiser and died a short time later. Following the crash, he made no attempt to help the officer. When questioned by police he gave them a false ID. It was later learned that Vivas-Diaz was in the United States illegally. An investigation by Phoenix Police showed that Vivas-Diaz was impaired by alcohol.
>
> On March 23, 2009, Vivas-Diaz pled guilty to manslaughter, a class 2 felony. He was sentenced on June 26, 2009, by Judge Michael Kemp. Deputy County Attorney Allister Adel prosecuted the case.
>
> Thomas stated, "Drunk driving often has deadly consequences. The consequences of Vivas-Diaz's actions claimed the life of a brave Phoenix Police Officer who died protecting the community. We honor the memory of Shane Figueroa." [2]

Officer Figueroa had been with the Phoenix Police Department for two years when he was killed. He left behind a wife and a 3-month-old baby.

43

Brittany Williams and Naomi Mercury

Age(s): 24 and 18, respectively
Location of Death: Raleigh, North Carolina
Killer: Mateo Palacio-Guzman

On November 3, 2014, police in Raleigh arrested Mateo Palacio-Guzman, 32, after he reportedly crashed his SUV into another vehicle, and fled the scene. Two passengers in the other vehicle were killed.

About 12:30 a.m., the illegal alien ran a red light at the intersection of New Bern Avenue and Trawick Road, smashing his truck into a Honda with five people inside, according to police.

Brittany Williams, of Fuquay-Varina, and Naomi Mercury, of Wake Forest, both died at the scene, while Nathan Lee Norris, Jr., 33, of Raleigh, and Tyrone Daniels, 26, of Raleigh, were both injured in the crash and transported to local hospitals.

After the crash, Palacio-Guzman actually continued smashing into the crumpled Honda as he tried to drive away.

Witness, Angel Turner, told WTVD:

> I saw him pretty much try to bum rush the car over so he could leave the scene. I could see he was actually damaging his car more as he was pushing the car out of the way, so I was taking note of that so I could give police a good description.[1]

When police caught up to the illegal alien at his Raleigh home, they found the damaged SUV being loaded onto a tow truck, in another attempt to hide his deadly crime.

Palacio-Guzman was charged with two counts of misdemeanor death by motor vehicle, driving while license suspended, failing to stop at a red light, and two counts of felony hit-and-run. He was booked into the Wake County Detention Center on an Immigration and Customs Enforcement (ICE) detainer.

Prior to the fatal crash, Palacio-Guzman had actually been deported three times—once in 2006, and twice in 2012. He had also been previously arrested for DUI in Wake County.

Shortly after the illegal alien's arrest, Wake County Sheriff Donnie Harrison recently voiced his frustration with the Obama administration, saying:

> Here we've done our job to try and get them back where they belong or let them go through the process that they need to go through to be here legally, and they haven't done that, they choose to keep coming back.... No help from the federal government whatsoever.
>
> How can we strengthen that? We can't, unless we get some better help from the federal government.[2]

Williams and Mercury were both students at Wake Technical Community College, where Mercury was studying psychology.

On August 2, 2016, Palacio-Guzman pleaded guilty to two counts of hit-and-run causing death, and was sentenced to five years and three months in prison.

He is currently housed at the Lumberton Correctional Insitute, with a projected release date of May 8, 2018, according to the North Carolina Department of Public Safety.[3]

44

Officer Henry Canales

Age: 42
Location of Death: Houston, Texas
Killer: Roberto Carillo

On June 23, 2009, Officer Canales was working undercover while assigned to an operation targeting a group of individuals trafficking in stolen merchandise.

ODMP reported:

> He and another officer were meeting with a group of suspects in a drugstore parking lot. As money was exchanged one of the suspects opened fire, fatally wounding Officer Canales. Another officer returned fire, killing the suspect. The three other suspects fled but were apprehended a short time later.[1]

The illegal alien who shot Officer Canales to death, was later identified as Roberto Carrillo.

Carrillo was deported in 1999 and had actually been ticketed four times since 2002, but was never reported to federal immigration authorities due to Houston's "sanctuary policy."

On June 26, 2009, Rep. Ted Poe (R-TX) made a speech on the floor of the U.S. House of Representatives about Officer Canales.

What follows is a portion of those remarks:

> Chief of Police Harold Hurtt said Canales "was not only an outstanding officer but an outstanding individual." He cared a great deal about his family, the people he worked with, and, of course, the City of Houston that he served.
>
> Madam Chair, I spent 30 years at the courthouse in Houston, Texas, as a prosecutor and as a judge. I have known hundreds of Houston police officers. They are the finest caliber and strongest of character, and Officer Canales was a rare breed in our culture who wore the badge to defend and protect the rest of us.
>
> Officer Canales died during surgery at the hospital where he and his family and hundreds of other officers had gathered. He was 42 years of age. This is a photograph of Officer Canales. He leaves behind his wife, Amor, a 15-year-old son, and a 17-year-old daughter....
>
> All Americans should recognize the profound debt of gratitude we owe our law enforcement officers and also the gratitude we owe their families. These officers put themselves into harm's way to guard our safety because they care about our communities and the people they serve. They are the ones standing between us and the bad guys every single day.
>
> So tonight we bid farewell with humble gratitude to Senior Officer Henry Canales. And to his wife, Amor, and his children, we say: May the Lord bless you and keep you. May His face shine upon you and be gracious to you. May He lift up His countenance upon you and give you peace. [2]

Officer Canales was a veteran of the U.S. Air Force, and served with the Houston Police Department for 16 years. He left behind a wife, a son, and a daughter.

45

Earl Olander

Age: 90
Location of Death: Carver County, Minnesota
Killer(s): Edson Celin-Dominguez Benitez
and Reinol Godines Vergara

On April 8, 2015, 90-year-old Earl Olander was found beaten to death inside his rural home.

On May 9, Carver County sheriff's deputies arrested Edson Celin-Dominguez Benitez, 29, and the next day, took Reinol Godiness Vergara, 35, into custody for the murder.

In 2014, the pair were hired by Olander to paint his house, and the bloody crime appeared to be one of opportunity, as Vergara said he knew that the old man would be "an easy target," according to detectives.[1]

Benitez and Vergara walked into Olander's home, and found him asleep on the sofa. They wrapped a blanket around his head and beat the 90-year-old repeatedly with the butt of a shotgun.

Olander bled to death with his hands duct-taped behind his back, as the assailants burglarized his home. Rare coins, silverware, savings bonds, and a foreign language Bible were stolen, among other items.

KARE 11 reported:

> It was that stolen bible that eventually led investigators to crack the case. Police received a call from a citizen who was cleaning out an apartment in St. Paul when he found the bible and two savings bonds issued to Earl Olander.

> The man searched Olander's name on the internet, found he had been the victim of homicide, and called authorities. Detectives then learned the apartment had been rented by Edson Benitez, located the suspect, and arrested him at his place of work.
>
> He admitted that he had been in possession of the bible, and had left it behind when he moved out. At the time of his arrest police say Edson was wearing a Croc shoe similar to one that left prints on the murder scene.[2]

Apparently, under questioning, Benitez told investigators of Vergara's role in the murder.

Both Benitez and Vergara were charged with second-degree murder and second-degree murder while committing a felony.

In May 2016, both illegal aliens pleaded guilty and were each sentenced to 37 years in prison. Both will be deported upon completion of their sentences.

46

Drew Rosenberg

Age: 25
Location of Death: San Francisco, California
Killer: Roberto Galo

On November 16, 2010, Rosenberg, a second-year law student, was riding his motorcycle home from classes when he was hit by unlicensed illegal alien Roberto Galo. In fact, the illegal alien not only hit the young man once, but actually backed up and ran over Rosenberg again, crushing the victim's abdomen, in an attempt to flee the scene. The only reason Galo actually stopped and was taken into custody was due to the brave actions of another motorist.[1]

Later that day, the Rosenbergs, who live in Los Angeles, were notified by staff at San Francisco General Hospital that Drew had been killed in a car accident.

Only six months earlier Galo had been charged with driving without a license, driving the wrong way on a one-way street, and driving without insurance.[2]

On July 27, 2010, Galo appeared in court to answer for the June violations. The DA's office made a deal with the illegal alien from Honduras...in exchange for pleading guilty to driving the wrong way on a one-way street, the charges of driving without a license and driving without insurance would be dropped.

Despite the lack of a driver's license, Galo continued to drive on San Francisco's streets, which would eventually lead to the grisly death of Drew Rosenberg, along with the bright future the young man had ahead of him.

In response to their son's death, the Rosenbergs started the website "Unlicensed to Kill," and have become activists in the fight to end "sanctuary policies," as well as demanding that the federal government actually enforce the nation's immigration laws.

The website states:

> Unlicensed to Kill was started to bring attention to the horrendous problem of unlicensed drivers who have no regard for the law and are responsible for death and destruction on our roads and highways every day. Last year 7,500 people were killed by unlicensed drivers.
>
> After my son was killed by an unlicensed driver in November 2010 I started to research the issue. I was stunned at what I found. Not only were unlicensed drivers killing people in numbers only exceeded by drunk drivers, but many times they were barely being punished and many times faced no charges at all.
>
> There are two different kinds of unlicensed drivers. There are those who have never been issued a license and those whose licensed has been suspended, revoked, or expired. Over 90 percent of those who have never been issued a license are in this country illegally....
>
> Despite all of this death and destruction very little is being done nationally, and in California many cities and

> the state are actually reducing the penalties and making it easier for unlicensed drivers to drive. While Unlicensed to Kill's main focus is on those who have never been issued a license, the two are inextricably linked (as are DUIs) and hopefully our efforts will spur individuals, groups, and our governmental agencies to take this problem seriously and begin to get these people off the roads.
>
> Over 20 people a day are killed by unlicensed drivers. It's time to put a stop to this slaughter.[3]

Six district attorneys later, and nearly two years after Drew was killed, on August 16, 2012, Galo was sentenced by the judge to six months in jail and three years' probation for vehicular manslaughter.

The Rosenbergs were not allowed to make an impact statement.

On April 4, 2013, Roberto Galo was deported to Honduras. His girlfriend (also an illegal alien) and their two children left the country a few days earlier, on March 29.

As of today, it is anybody's guess as to the whereabouts of Roberto Galo.

Drew, Don, and Evan Rosenberg

47

Officer David Hofer

Age: 29
Location of Death: Euless, Texas
Killer: Jorge Brian Gonzalez

On March 1, 2016, Jorge Brian Gonzalez shot to death Officer Hofer in Texas, while the illegal alien was apparently high on methamphetamine.

Hofer, along with other officers, was responding to reports of a suspicious person and shots fired at J.A. Carr Park when the deadly shooting took place. "Upon arrival, officers encountered a suspect with an unknown weapon," [Euless Police Chief Mike] Brown said. "The suspect immediately fired upon officers, striking one of them. Officers returned fire, striking the suspect," reported WFAA.[1]

Officer Hofer was transported to Baylor Scott & White Medical Center, where he quickly died from his wounds.

The Dallas Morning News reported:

> Gonzalez was arrested in April 2011 on a charge of theft from a person. It was the start of a string of arrests for thefts, assaults, and making terroristic threats. Every arrest occurred in Euless, except for a Fort Worth case of assault causing bodily injury to a family member last March, records show.
>
> His father called Fort Worth police last year to an apartment on East Loop 820 after Gonzalez threatened his father and his sister Jennifer with a knife. He had also

> hit his sister with a 1-by-4-inch board, according to the police report. The father told police that his son was on drugs and violent, the report says.
>
> In November 2015, Gonzales was accused of theft and criminal mischief of between $100 and $750, records show. He pleaded guilty to the criminal mischief charge and was convicted around the same time as for the theft charge.
>
> He was released from the Tarrant County jail January 11. At most, Gonzalez was sentenced to 90 days in jail for his past crimes.[2]

Brian Gonzalez's rap sheet includes: a July 2011 theft charge, an August 2011 aggravated assault with a deadly weapon charge that was reduced to a misdemeanor assault charge on a guilty plea, and two terrorist threat charges in summer 2015.

Gonzalez, who came to this country illegally from Argentina, was shot to death by Officer Hofer's partner.

Officer Hofer served with the Euless Police Department for two years, and previously served with the New York City Police Department for five years, according to ODMP.[3]

48

Grant Ronnebeck

Age: 21
Location of Death: Mesa, Arizona
Killer: Apolinar Altamirano

On January 22, 2015, a store surveillance camera captured the images of Apolinar Altamirano, 29, fatally shooting Ronnebeck, the clerk at the QuickTrip convenience store in Mesa, Arizona, near the intersection of Stapley and Broadway.

Ronnebeck, had worked in the store since high school. Altamirano apparently shot Ronnebeck after growing impatient with the amount of time the transaction was taking. The illegal alien asked for a pack of cigarettes and then dumped a pile of coins on the counter.

Ronnebeck fell dead behind the counter, and Altamirano stepped over him, helping himself to more cigarettes before walking out of the store, according to police.

Altamirano fled the scene in his car, leading police officers on a 25-mile, high-speed chase that ended when the suspect crashed his vehicle at the intersection of 19th Avenue and Buckeye Road. Two guns were found inside the car.

Altamirano had actually been banned from entering the store two weeks before the shooting.

The Arizona Republic reported:

> Apolinar Altamirano had been told to stay out of the QuikTrip at Stapley Drive and Broadway Road, in central Mesa, on January 9, the document said.[1]

> "I think he had been at the store previously and there was a disturbance," said Detective Steve Berry, a Mesa police spokesman. "He was told he was not allowed in the store."[2]

Altamirano was charged with first-degree murder, felony flight, and armed robbery.

While all crimes committed by illegal aliens are 100 percent preventable (with only a secure border and immigration laws which are enforced), this murder is doubly maddening, as Altamirano pleaded guilty to burglary in 2012 and should have been deported.

On July 21, 2015, Grant's uncle, Michael Ronnebeck testified before the U.S. Senate Judiciary Committee. A portion of that testimony follows:

> At 4:00 a.m. on January 22, 2015, just six months ago, while working the overnight shift at his Quiktrip store, Grant assisted a man buying cigarettes. The man dumped a jar of coins on the counter and demanded cigarettes. Grant tried explaining that he needed to count the coins before he could give the man the cigarettes.
>
> The man then pulled a gun, and stated "you're not gonna take my money," and "you're not gonna give me my cigarettes." Grant immediately offered up the cigarettes to the man, who shot him in the face point blank, killing him. Seemingly unaffected, the man coldly and callously stepped over Grant's dying body, grabbed a couple of packs of cigarettes, and then left the store.
>
> After a 30-minute high speed pursuit through the streets of Mesa and Phoenix, Arizona, the man was taken

> into custody. Inside his car were the cigarettes and two handguns, one believed to be the gun used to kill Grant. Apolinar Altamirano, the alleged murderer, is an illegal alien.
>
> According to a news article detailing his 2012 arrest, he is a self-proclaimed member of the Mexican mafia, and says he has ties to the Sinaloa drug cartel. The news article states that in August of 2012, he was arrested with two others after kidnapping and sexually assaulting a woman and burglarizing her apartment.
>
> She was allegedly held naked and against her will for a full week prior to escaping. He took a plea deal, and pled guilty to a charge of felony burglary for that incident.... It is my family's greatest desire that Grant Ronnebeck's legacy will be more than a fading obituary, a cemetery plot, or a fond memory. Instead, we want Grant's death to be a force for change and reform in the immigration policies of this great nation.[3]

Grant left behind his parents Steven Ronnebeck, Sandy Kemps, and Jill Kirkpatrick, along with two brothers and a sister.

After his murder, Grant's family started the Grant Ronnebeck Foundation, with its primary goals being to "raise awareness and to provide immediate financial assistance for burial costs, emotional support resources to any families that lost a loved one to a crime commited by an illegal alien."[4]

49

William "Dennis" McCann

Age: 66
Location of Death: Chicago, Illinois
Killer: Saul Chavez

On June 8, 2011, McCann was walking in a crosswalk in Chicago when he was mowed down by Saul Chavez, 36, driving a Dodge Neon. Chavez hit the victim, then dragged his body, still lodged beneath the car, for a whole block, and only stopped after a police officer drew his weapon on the Mexican national.

Chavez had a blood alcohol concentration of 0.29 percent when he killed McCann, according to court records. He was also convicted of a DUI in 2009, and was actually on probation at the time.

For McCann's death, he was charged with aggravated DUI causing death. Immigration and Customs Enforcement (ICE) issued a detainer for Chavez, but because Cook County has a sanctuary policy for illegal aliens, Chavez was allowed to bond out, and fled to Mexico.[1]

On July 21, 2015, the victim's brother, Brian McCann, testified before the U.S. Senate Judiciary Committee.

An excerpt from that testimony follows:

> On behalf of the McCann family I want to thank you, Senator [Chuck] Grassley, [R-IA]and the other members of the Judiciary Committee for this opportunity to share with you my efforts to return justice to our family after the violent death of my brother Denny on June 8, 2011, in Chicago, Illinois. Denny was crossing Kedzie Avenue on a marked crosswalk four years ago and was violently struck by a drunk driver who dragged Denny under his car for a block in an attempt to flee before Denny died. The family was notified by the Chicago Police and the killer was placed into custody and charged with aggravated DUI causing death. Two days later ICE issued a detainer because the young man was an illegal alien with a prior felony.
>
> The family was assured by the Cook County prosecutor that the defendant would not be allowed to post bail and be released. Three months later the Cook County Board passed the ordinance that effectively requires the Sheriff to ignore detainers. During the intervening weeks after Denny's violent death, Cook County President Toni Preckwinkle and former mayoral candidate and Commissioner Jesus Garcia pushed for the ordinance and rammed it through on September 7, 2011.
>
> Two months later the killer made bail and absconded to Mexico. Perhaps the most disturbing aspect of this whole ordeal was that we also learned that this illegal alien was prosecuted for another felony two years earlier and ICE was never notified then. He was removed from probation February 2011 and four months later killed Denny.
>
> In short Denny would be alive today and enjoying the birth of a new granddaughter born two weeks ago if the Cook County criminal justice system that included the county board did their job. I received confirmation that he is indeed in Mexico from the FBI and is currently driving a truck. I had to prevail on my Congressman to get the FBI to cooperate with my request for information and action. I have not heard from the Bureau in over six months.[2]
>
> McCann left behind two daughters and was predeceased by his son, Justin.[3]

50

Dimitri Smith

Age: Infant
Location of Death: Santa Fe, New Mexico
Killer: Ramon Hernandez

On June 10, 2012, Zach and Aileen Smith were traveling along Interstate 25 in San Miguel County when a vehicle driven by Ramon Hernandez, 43, crashed into their car.

Aileen Smith suffered severe contusions to her midsection as well as a broken sternum. She was seven months pregnant with the couple's first child.

Dimitri was delivered by C-section, but any hopes of the baby boy's survival were quickly dashed.

"Dimitri lived for about a minute, I was told," said Aileen Smith. "He died of a massive head injury and blood on the brain," reported KOAT.[1]

It was the illegal alien's fifth DUI.

According to the New Mexico State Motor Vehicle Division, Hernandez was convicted of DUI twice in 2000, once in 2003, and again in 2004. He was driving on a revoked license at the time of the fatal crash. His license was reportedly suspended due to unpaid traffic tickets.

Hernandez was originally charged with felony DWI and causing injury to a pregnant woman, but after further consideration Las Vegas, N.M., District Attorney Richard Flores added the charge of vehicular homicide.[2]

Ramon Hernandez was convicted of vehicular homicide and causing great bodily injury to a pregnant woman, and sentenced to nine years in prison.

Unfortunately, the conviction was thrown out by the New Mexico Court of Appeals on a technicality.[3]

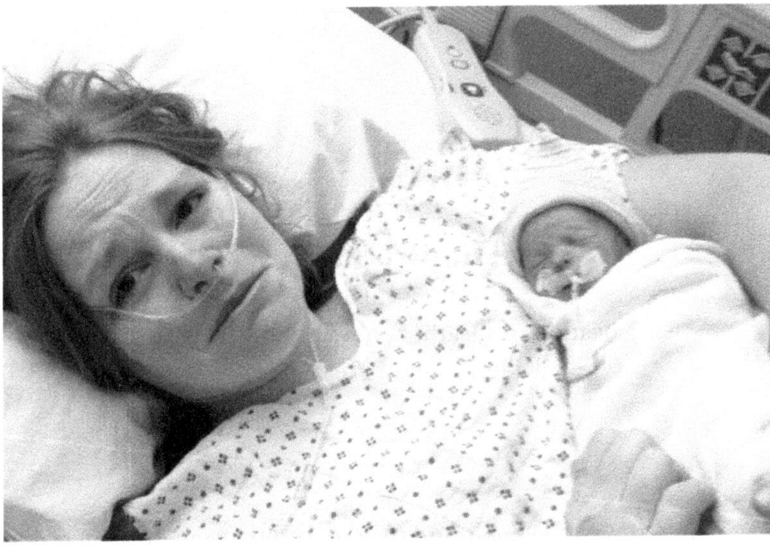

AFTERWORD

The tragic fate of the individuals documented in this book—the senseless, premature loss of life—is that their unfortunate deaths *could* have been and *should* have been prevented *if U.S. immigration laws had been properly enforced.*

These Americans did not perish in a foreign war, though they did die violently. You might say that they died in a different kind of war. For those lost, there are no wreath-laying ceremonies, no twenty-one gun salutes nor community gatherings.

Those who are left behind truly suffer in silence, as local media sources often refer to the illegal alien charged with a homicide as "a Raleigh man," or simply as "a man," or just omitting any mention of these killers' immigration status.

Contrary to what the mainstream press most often claims, a criminal's illegal status in this country is completely relevant to the case. You see, unlike nearly all other crimes, those committed by illegal aliens are 100 percent preventable.

It's really very simple: *if they are not here, they are not here to commit the crime*!

Despite the rhetoric coming from many local officials, claiming that they have no legal role in enforcing our immigration laws, that is simply a lie. In 1996, the Illegal Immigration Reform and Immigrant Responsibility Act (IIRIRA) was passed as a federal law which requires local governments to cooperate with ICE. The local governments that have been enforcing their own "sanctuary" policies are actually defying this law.

U.S. citizens have a right, according to the Constitution, to expect to be protected from violations of federal law by foreign nationals, who are not authorized to be in the country, without local authorities aiding and abetting these criminal aliens in their unlawful activities.

It is important that all of us understand the devastating impact that illegal immigration is having upon our nation, and particularly upon those families who have lost loved ones due to the criminal actions of those here illegally. It is equally important to understand that the lawmakers and various public officials, by their inaction in removing those illegal aliens, are every bit as culpable for those deaths as are the illegal aliens who get behind the wheel drunk every day in this country.

It is a cold, hard slap in the face to these families for any politician to consider or even speak publicly about passing any form of amnesty for illegal aliens.

May the memories of every American killed by an illegal alien forever haunt those who have enabled this deadly invasion.

APPENDIX
How Much Crime Do Illegal Aliens Commit?

Recently, advocates and apologists for illegal aliens have been using the talking point ad nauseam: "immigrants commit less crime than native-born Americans." While it is true that, by and large, "immigrants" are law-abiding folks, *illegal aliens* are not "immigrants"; by the very nature of their presence in this nation, they are criminals.

A daily example of the "culture" we are importing from South of the Border can be found in the virtual "border state" of North Carolina.

In just one month (April 2014) illegal aliens committed more than 390 sex crimes against children across the state of North Carolina, or an average of 13 a day. In fact, between January 1, 2014, and June 15, 2015, 5,675 charges of child sexual assault were filed against illegal aliens in the Tarheel State, according to the law enforcement advocacy group known as NCFIRE.[1]

Though the Obama administration wanted us to believe that every illegal alien in this country is either a "valedictorian" or an upstanding "New American" who only wants to work and build a better life for his family, the facts paint a much different picture.

On April 14, 2015, Sarah Saldana, Director of U.S. Immigration and Customs Enforcement (ICE), appeared before the House Judiciary Committee, and some stark revelations about the lawlessness of the Obama administration came to light.

- Between fiscal years 2013 and 2014, ICE released 66,565 illegal aliens who were previously convicted of crimes in this country.
- Those criminal aliens accounted for nearly 30,000 DUIs, 2,600 incidents of domestic violence, 800 sexual assaults, nearly 500 kidnappings, and 300 murders.

You see, under President Obama, ICE agents were no longer allowed to arrest and deport illegal aliens for simply being in this country illegally, and the citizens he swore to protect were all too often the victims of this policy.

Unfortunately, until very recently, the federal government rarely released any hard data on the number of crimes committed by illegal aliens, but that has changed with the Trump administration.

On June 7, 2018, the U.S. Department of Justice (DOJ) released a report which revealed the rather startling fact that *one in five of those incarcerated in federal prisons are foreign nationals*, of whom 93 percent are here illegally. This comes at a cost of nearly $1.5 million a day to U.S. taxpayers.

The report stated:

> A total of 57,820 known or suspected aliens were in DOJ custody at the end of FY 2018 Q1, including 38,132 persons in BOP [Bureau of Prisons] custody and 19,688 in USMS [U.S. Marshals Service] custody. Of this total, 42,284 people had been confirmed by U.S. Immigration and Customs Enforcement (ICE) to be aliens (i.e., non-citizens and non-nationals), while 15,536 aliens were still under investigation by ICE to determine alienage and/or removability.
>
> Among the 42,284 confirmed aliens, 39,413 people (93 percent) were unlawfully present. These numbers include a 62 percent unlawful rate among 38,132 known or suspected aliens in BOP custody and a 78 percent unlawful rate among 19,688 confirmed aliens in USMS custody.
>
> Approximately 16,233 aliens in USMS custody required housing in state, local, and private facilities, which cost $1,458,372.72 a day.[2]

That same report stated that between 2011 and 2018, more than 660,000 criminal aliens had run afoul of the law *in Texas alone*. These findings also included this admonition: "These data do not account for all aliens in the Texas criminal justice system, as they are limited to criminal alien arrestees who have had prior interaction with DHS [Department of Homeland Security] resulting in the collection of their fingerprints."

The section on Texas gave the following breakdown on crimes committed by aliens in the state:

> 1,351 homicides; 7,156 sexual assaults; 9,938 weapons charges; 79,049 assaults; 18,685 burglaries; 79,900 drug charges; 815 kidnappings; 44,882 thefts; 4,292 robberies.

Furthermore, on June 22, 2018, the White House released the following statistics on crimes perpetrated by illegal aliens:

> The Victims of Immigration Crime Engagement Office (VOICE) has released a new report that includes case studies explaining how they were able to assist victims who contacted them.
>
> A 2011 Government Accountability Office report found nearly 3 million offenses tied to criminal aliens, including:
>
> More than 25,000 homicide offenses.
>
> More than 42,000 robbery offenses.
>
> Nearly 70,000 sex crime offenses.
>
> Nearly 15,000 kidnapping offenses.
>
> In Texas alone, more than 250,000 criminal aliens have been arrested and charged with over 600,000 criminal offenses within the last seven years.
>
> In fiscal year 2017, more than 8,000 criminal illegal aliens in police custody were released back into our communities as a result of sanctuary policies.[3]

Over the next few years, as more data are accrued, we will bear witness to the true scope of the danger to which every president following Dwight D. Eisenhower has allowed Americans citizens to be subjected.[4]

Just how many violent aliens—murderers, rapists, and assorted felons—are an *acceptable* number to allow across our borders and victimize our fellow citizens?

APPENDIX ENDNOTES

1. http://www.ncfire.info/

2. https://www.justice.gov/opa/pr/departments-justice-and-homeland-security-release-quarterly-alien-incarceration-report

3. https://www.whitehouse.gov/briefings-statements/president-donald-j-trump-stands-victims-illegal-alien-crime/

4. https://tshaonline.org/handbook/online/articles/pqo01

ENDNOTES

Chapter 1

1. http://pilotonline.com/news/virginia-beach-leaders-strike-back-at-fox-s-bill-o/article_78e155ab-9336-52a1-a210-2
2. http://www.washingtontimes.com/news/2007/apr/15/20070415-104656-5932r/) 0e7655ee4901.html
3. http://www.foxnews.com/opinion/2010/08/10/ray-tranchant-daughter-killed-viriginia-beach-dui-illegal-immigrant-mexico.html

[Note: misspelling of Virginia above appears in original link.]

4. https://vadoc.virginia.gov/offenders/locator/results.aspx

Chapter 2

1. https://outerbanksvoice.com/2012/12/10/justice-awaits-capture-of-driver-in-fatal-2011-crash/

Chapter 3

1.http://www.pe.com/articles/tzun-655699-driving-license.html

2.http://politicalhotwire.com/current-events/126464-another-obama-dreamer-proves-trump-may-right-25.html

3. http://www.pe.com/articles/enforcement-773765-ice-immigration.html
4. http://www.domhugs.com/
5. https://rcc.academicworks.com/opportunities/2959

Chapter 4

1. https://www.thedenverchannel.com/news/family-buries-boy-killed-in-ice-cream-crash
2. https://www.summitdaily.com/news/family-grapples-with-3-year-olds-death/

Chapter 5

1. http://www.omaha.com/news/crime/saddest-day-of-my-life-at-dui-sentencing-words-of/article_c25db86e-e920-11e4-855e-7fbd45fbe7fc.html
2. http://www.ice.gov/doclib/detention-reform/pdf/detainer-policy.pdf
3. http://www.wowt.com/home/headlines/Pedestrian-Struck-By-Hit-And-Run-Driver-264171181.html

Chapter 6

1. http://www.chron.com/news/houston-texas/article/HPD-officer-dies-after-traffic-stop-turns-tragic-1519107.php

2. http://www.chron.com/news/houston-texas/article/Houston-businessman-pleads-guilty-to-harboring-1735288.php

3. http://www.odmp.org/officer/18510-officer-rodney-joseph-johnson

Chapter 7

1. http://www.leagle.com/decision/1984462322SE2d140_1458.xml/STATE%20v.%20ZUNIGA

2. https://www.ncdps.gov/our-organization/adult-correction/prisons/death-penalty/list-removed-death-row

3. http://www.deathpenaltyinfo.org/foreign-nationals-part-iii

4. http://law.justia.com/cases/north-carolina/supreme-court/1987/156a85-0-0.html

5. https://webapps.doc.state.nc.us/opi/offendersearch.do?method=view

Chapter 8

1. https://www.odmp.org/officer/16353-park-ranger-kristopher-william-eggle

Chapter 9

1. http://www.telegram.com/article/20100806/NEWS/100809795

2. http://www.legacy.com/obituaries/milforddailynews/obituary.aspx?pid=134794926

Chapter 10

1. http://www.timesdispatch.com/news/state-regional/substitute-minister-sentenced-to-years-in-crash-that-killed-newspaper/article_264f1ac3-f25f-552f-a870-242db1c687d0.html

2. http://www.nytimes.com/2012/04/28/us/politics/traffic-violations-wont-earn-illegal-immigrants-deportation.html?ref=us&_r=1&

3. http://judiciary.house.gov/hearings/Hearings%202012/hear_03072012_2.html

4. http://www.legacy.com/obituaries/name/maxey-lynch-obituary?pid=1000000164140505&view=guestbook

Chapter 11

1. https://web.archive.org/web/20070406152453/http://www.latimes.com/news/local/la-me-crash5apr05%2C0%2C6240856.story?coll=la-home-headlines

2. http://www.eonline.com/news/56434/prison-for-driver-in-fatal-director-crash

Chapter 12

1. http://www.imdb.com/name/nm6663204/

2. http://www.wbtv.com/story/28215256/slain-top-model-contestant-spoke-against-violence

3. http://www.charlotteobserver.com/news/local/crime/article142584879.html

Chapter 13

1. http://archive.boston.com/news/local/massachusetts/articles/2011/08/22/driver_in_fatal_milford_hit_and_run_to_be_arraigned/

2. http://www.legacy.com/obituaries/name/matthew-denice-obituary?pid=178664310&view=guestbook

Chapter 14

1. http://www.fox10phoenix.com/story/26639959/2014/09/26/man-gets-8-year-prison-sentence-in-death-of-phoenix-police-officer

2. http://www.odmp.org/officer/21784-police-officer-daryl-michael-raetz

3. https://arizonadailyindependent.com/2013/06/04/hit-an-run-driver-arrested-in-death-of-phoenix-policeman/

Chapter 15

1. http://www.washingtonpost.com/wp-dyn/content/article/2010/08/02/AR2010080205264_2.html?sid=ST2010101406785

2. http://www.pwcgov.org/news/pages/pr02162011ice.aspx

Chapter 16

1. http://www.browardpalmbeach.com/news/report-released-on-driver-accused-in-hit-and-run-death-of-10-year-old-6467570

Chapter 17

1. http://fox13now.com/2017/05/18/man-sentenced-to-life-in-prison-for-killing-millard-co-deputy/

2. http://archive.sltrib.com/article.php?id=5305331&itype=CMSID

Chapter 18

1. http://www.mysanantonio.com/news/local_news/article/Grief-grips-neighborhood-4223085.php

2. http://www.mysanantonio.com/news/local_news/article/Grand-jury-halts-prosecution-of-teen-driver-who-4493061.php

3. http://news4sanantonio.com/news/local-deprecated/texting-while-driving-ban-dies-in-legislature

Chapter 19

1. http://www.omaha.com/article/20130724/NEWS/130729475/1707

2. http://journalstar.com/news/state-and-regional/nebraska/murder-charge-filed-after--year-old-rape-victim-dies/article_026ec141-96ed-52a4-9f32-6cc31239bd42.html

3. http://www.wowt.com/home/headlines/Suspect-Pleads-Guilty-Sentenced-To-Life-For-Murder-Of-Elderly-Woman-254546371.html

Chapter 20

1. https://montgomerycountypolicereporter.com/dwi-driver-who-killed-13-year-old-sentenced/

2. http://abc13.com/archive/7315462/

Chapter 21

1. https://www.americasfreedomfighters.com/2014/05/17/obamas-drunken-illegal-aliens-another-murdered-police-officer/

2. http://www.azdps.gov/Media/News/View/?p=476

3. http://www.azfamily.com/story/25498630/fallen-mesa-officer-a-man-of-many-passions

Chapter 22

1. https://www.c-span.org/person/?angiemorfin

2. http://www.breitbart.com/california/2015/11/01/murdered-illegal-aliens-2015-families-gather-remembrance/

Chapter 23

1. https://pilotonline.com/news/local/crime/archive-police-officers-killed-in-line-of-duty-since/article_ed9aff62-6c29-533a-9d77-5368e4abcd9a.html

2. http://www.odmp.org/officer/16512-police-officer-sheila-herring

Chapter 24

1. http://www.masscops.com/threads/woman-sentenced-in-fatal-school-bus-crash-case.63036/

2. http://www.norcraftcabinetry.com/

3. https://bailbondcity.com/minnesota/mndoc-inmate-Morales/227521

Chapter 25

1. http://azcapitoltimes.com/news/2011/03/28/krentzs-murder-still-unsolved-after-year/

2. http://www.fronterasdesk.org/content/9181/arizona-sheriff-person-interest-krentz-murder-local

3. https://arizonadailyindependent.com/2016/03/15/sue-krentz-its-all-irrelative-until-it-is-your-relative/

4. http://www.wmicentral.com/news/latest_news/sue-krentz-recovering-from-pedestrian-accident/article_3ef13d78-ccee-11df-badb-001cc4c002e0.html

Chapter 26

1.http://www.oregon.gov/osp/pages/bret_clodfelter.aspx

2. https://www.klamathcounty.org/490/Public-Safety

Chapter 27

1. https://web.archive.org/web/20080722113525/2. http://www.sfgate.com/cgi-bin/article.cgi?f=%2Fc%2Fa%2F2008%2F07%2F20%2FMNK011MAFR.DTL

2. http://sanfrancisco.cbslocal.com/2012/01/25/surviving-son-testifies-in-2008-bologna-family-killings/

3. http://www.sfgate.com/crime/article/SF-killer-Edwin-Ramos-sentenced-in-triple-slaying-3625545.php

4. http://www.sfgate.com/bayarea/article/Judge-tosses-sanctuary-suit-in-S-F-killings-3198588.php

Chapter 28

1. http://amwfans.com/thread/827/gonzalo-harrell-gonzalez-georgia-2000

2. http://www.cbs46.com/story/32248778/man-in-country-illegally-accused-of-killing-teen-likely-wont-be-jailed

3. http://www.thedustininmansociety.org/index.html

Chapter 29

1. http://www.fncic-voiacm.org/victims.php?id=1048

2. http://www.legacy.com/obituaries/jsonline/obituary.aspx?pid=111729074

Chapter 30

1. http://www.nonpareilonline.com/news/local/felony-arrest-warrant-issued-for-eswin-mejia/article_8169fe1e-f291-5ddb-a0f1-c3d73aedccb6.html

2. http://cis.org/Sanctuary-Cities-Map

3. http://www.radioiowa.com/2016/02/16/teen-charged-in-iowa-womans-death-mayve-fled-the-country/

4. http://www.wowt.com/home/headlines/Family-friends-mourn-Sarah-Roots-death--367988481.html

Chapter 31

1. http://www.buckeyeaz.gov/police/officer-memorial/

2. http://www.legacy.com/obituaries/azcentral/obituary.aspx?pid=150773437

Chapter 32

1. https://www.click2houston.com/news/police-classmate-confesses-to-killing-teen-burning-body

2. http://www.chron.com/news/houston-texas/houston/article/21-year-old-convicted-in-beating-death-of-former-4233272.php

3. https://www.c-span.org/video/?327240-1/hearing-immigration-enforcement

Chapter 33

1. http://laspa.org/services/memorium/david_march.htm

2. http://ktla.com/2016/04/29/24-hour-vigil-held-for-sheriffs-deputy-killed-during-2002-traffic-stop-in-irwindale/

Chapter 34

1. http://www.sfgate.com/bayarea/article/Boy-4-killed-in-Santa-Rosa-hit-run-suspect-held-2334422.php

2. http://www.pressdemocrat.com/news/2483512-181/a-painful-poignant-thank-you?artslide=0

3. http://www.legacy.com/obituaries/sfgate/obituary.aspx?pid=153254880

Chapter 35

1. https://www.odmp.org/officer/19001-police-officer-nicki-james-nick-erfle

2. https://sympathy.legacy.com/en-us/funeral-flowers/name/nick-erfle-flowers/p94687467/

3. http://tucsoncitizen.com/morgue/2007/09/20/63438-cop-killed-by-migrant-who-d-been-deported/

Chapter 36

1. https://www.policearrests.com/arrests/abel_arango_id_5096412.html

2. http://archive.naplesnews.com/news/crime/authorities-tried-to-lock-up-deport-shooter-who-killed-fort-myers-police-officer-ep-401417301-344448372.html

3. http://www.nbc-2.com/story/10693582/statement-from-officer-widmans-family

Chapter 37

1. https://www.denverpost.com/2005/05/08/officer-dies-in-ambush/

2. https://www.denverpost.com/2006/10/25/gomez-garcia-gets-the-max-80-years/

Chapter 38

1. http://www.cyclerides.com/marc.htm

2. https://www.odmp.org/officer/15232-police-officer-marc-todd-atkinson

Chapter 39

1. http://clarkstonnews.com/trial-underway-in-drunk-driver-murder-case/

2. https://forum.officer.com/forum/public-forums/officer-down-news-memorials/74457-flint-mi-officer-down-8-26-07

3. http://illegalaliensrunningamuk.blogspot.com/2007/08/danna-vincent-owen.html

4. http://www.mlive.com/news/flint/index.ssf/2008/06/ramon_pineda_sentenced_to_2870.html

Chapter 40

1. http://www.wral.com/apncnews/7161933/detail.html

2. https://www.govtrack.us/congress/bills/112/hr3808/text/ih

3. https://judiciary.house.gov/_files/hearings/Hearings%202012/Myrick%2003072012.pdf

Chapter 41

1. http://articles.latimes.com/2008/mar/04/local/me-shot4

2. https://en.wikipedia.org/wiki/Special_Order_40

3. http://articles.latimes.com/2012/nov/02/local/la-me-1103-jamiel-shaw-20121104

4. https://drive.google.com/file/d/0BxdramCRlPl0NzdlYmNhNTktYjBkNi00ZTFmLWE4YjctYzY2NzA4ODJkYjUy/view

Chapter 42

1. https://www.odmp.org/officer/19621-police-officer-shane-cory-figueroa

2. https://mylifeofcrime.files.wordpress.com/2009/06/20090626_b-sentencing.pdf

Chapter 43

1. http://abc11.com/377016/

2. http://www.wakegov.com/sheriff/Pages/default.aspx

3. https://webapps.doc.state.nc.us/opi/offendersearch.do?method=view

Chapter 44

1. https://www.odmp.org/officer/19986-police-officer-henry-canales

2. https://poe.house.gov/floor-remarks?ID=D1BDFA81-6D52-446C-ABB2-FAD812128395

Chapter 45

1. http://minnesota.cbslocal.com/2016/05/06/2-twin-cities-men-sentenced-to-37-years-for-murder-of-elderly-farmer/

2. http://www.kare11.com/story/news/crime/2015/05/13/2-charged-in-murder-of-90-year-old-farmer/27237823/

Chapter 46

1. http://archive.vcstar.com/news/sons-death-fuels-westlake-village-mans-push-against-unlicensed-drivers-ep-363398262-352035771.html/

2. http://articles.latimes.com/2013/jan/26/local/la-me-0127-lopez-unlicensed-20130125

3. http://unlicensedtokill.org/the-story/

Chapter 47

1. http://www.wfaa.com/news/crime/euless-officer-shot-condition-unknown/63452116

2. http://crimeblog.dallasnews.com/2016/03/suspect-in-euless-officers-slaying-was-meth-addict-just-released-from-jail-tuesday-his-family-says.html/

3. https://www.odmp.org/officer/22792-police-officer-david-stefan-hofer

Chapter 48

1. https://www.pressreader.com/usa/the-arizona-republ ic/20150124/281573764095861

2. http://www.azcentral.com/story/news/local/mesa/2015/01/23/mesa-qt-murder-court-records-abrk/22219037/

3. http://www.judiciary.senate.gov/imo/media/doc/07-21-15%20 Ronnebeck%20Testimony.pd

4. https://www.thegrantronnebeckfoundation.org/the-project

Chapter 49

1. https://chicagocitywire.com/stories/511198503-activist-argues-sanctuary-status-makes-illinois-a-safe-place-for-criminals

2. http://www.judiciary.senate.gov/imo/media/doc/07-21-15%20 McCann%20Testimony.pdf

3. http://www.legacy.com/obituaries/chicagotribune/obituary. aspx?n=w-dennis-mccann&pid=151856662

Chapter 50

1. http://www.koat.com/article/smith-family-seeks-justice-in-death-of-their-first-born-son/5052616

2. https://www.abqjournal.com/121716/alleged-dwi-claims-tiny-life. html

3. http://www.lcsun-news.com/story/news/2016/12/31/conviction-tossed-collision-led-babys-death/96044902/